PAUL'S LIFE AND LETTERS

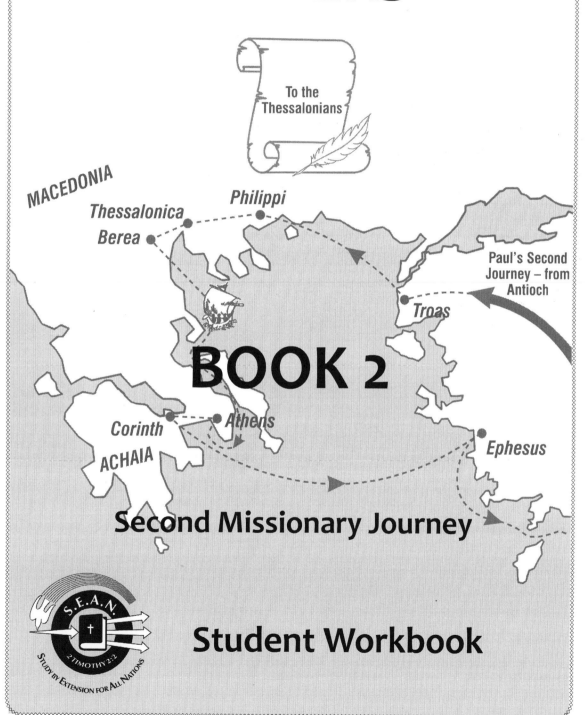

To the
Thessalonians

MACEDONIA

Thessalonica
Berea

Philippi

Paul's Second
Journey – from
Antioch

Troas

BOOK 2

Corinth
ACHAIA

Athens

Ephesus

Second Missionary Journey

S.E.A.N.
2 TIMOTHY 2:2
STUDY BY EXTENSION FOR ALL NATIONS

Student Workbook

MW01280065

SEAN International

SEAN (pronounced "Say-an") means Study by Extension for All Nations.

Paul's Life and Letters – Book 2 is the second of a series of three books which teach the themes of Paul's letters and present his life and missionary journeys in detail.

Each are intended to be studied in a group directed by a Group Leader who uses the accompanying Group Leader's Guide.

This SEAN course has been based on the New International Version of the Bible. If you use other versions, adjustments may be necessary.

Our website:
www.seaninternational.org

Our e-mail:
contact@seaninternational.org

First English Edition 1990
New Revised American English Edition 2021
ISBN: 978-1-899049-70-7

Contents

Introduction

This Book is the second in a series of three on "Paul's Life and Letters". The whole series is as follows.

Book 1   Paul's birth, early life, and first missionary journey, with his letter to the Galatians.

Book 2   The second missionary journey and the related letters, especially 1 and 2 Thessalonians.

Book 3   The third missionary journey, imprisonments and martyrdom, and related letters.

Welcome to Book 2 of our series on "Paul's Life and Letters". This course will focus on Paul's second missionary journey and the letters he wrote that are related to this journey. Read the objectives of this course given below.

Objectives of Book 2

On completing this book you will be able to

a)   describe the main events in Paul's second missionary journey, especially naming the five main towns where he ministered and the Roman provinces in which they were situated.

b)   name the two letters Paul wrote on his second journey, and explain how passages from these letters throw light on this period of Paul's life and ministry, and what he preached about in Thessalonica.

c)   name the letters Paul later wrote to the churches he founded on the second missionary journey, and explain how passages from these throw light on the events, places and people connected with his second journey.

d)   name Paul's companions on his second missionary journey and describe their movements and ministry during this period.

e)   name the letters Paul wrote at the end of his life to one of his companions of the second journey, and illustrate how these give much information both about this companion and also about Paul's methods for training people for ministry.

f)   apply Paul's teaching in your own life, service and ministry, as well as develop perseverance and trust in God in all situations.

g)   follow Paul's example in communicating biblical teaching to others so they, too, may be enabled to pass it on to others.

Instructions on How to Do the Lessons

1. **Lessons A, B** and **C** are to be completed at home by the students.

2. **Lessons C** are Group Bible Studies which will be reviewed in the weekly Group Meetings with the Group Leader and the rest of the students.

How to Use the Lessons for Research and Review

Research Instructions

1. As in Book 1, there are blank lines provided for you to write the answers to each numbered point, or boxes to check the correct answer. You can find the answers by looking up the place in the Bible or elsewhere as indicated in the reference at the end of the line.

2. You can, if you prefer, write the answers in a notebook with their numbering as given in the lesson, e.g. 1a) 1b) etc. In this way you will be able to review better.

3. After completing each numbered point, check, and if necessary correct, your answer(s) for that number. You will find the correct answers at the foot of the page. The answers to Lessons C are in the Group Leader's Guide and will be checked at the Group Meeting.

Remember:

First: Find the answer by looking up the reference, or by working it out.
Second: Write your answers in the blanks provided, or if you prefer, in a notebook.
Third: Complete each point before checking and then go on to the next one.

Review Instructions

4. Do the lesson once and then review by going through it again, making sure you have understood and learned the whole lesson well.

5. Once you are confident that you have mastered the contents you should do the test for the corresponding lesson. You will find these tests, starting on page 92 of this workbook.

6. Then, finally do Lesson C, but not the test which you will do at home after the Group Meeting.

Introductory Group Study
Jerusalem / Antioch United Project
(Acts 15:22–35)

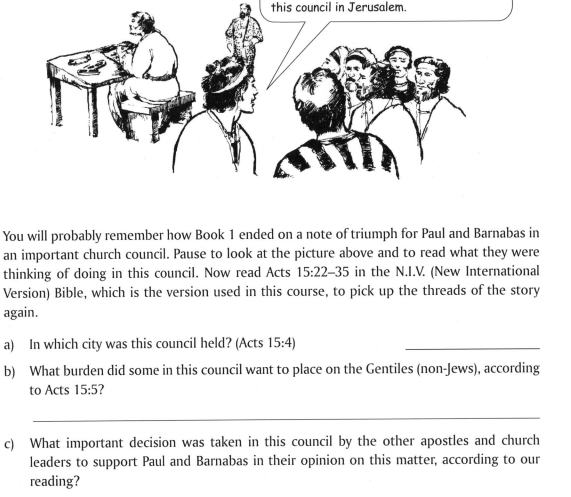

1. You will probably remember how Book 1 ended on a note of triumph for Paul and Barnabas in an important church council. Pause to look at the picture above and to read what they were thinking of doing in this council. Now read Acts 15:22–35 in the N.I.V. (New International Version) Bible, which is the version used in this course, to pick up the threads of the story again.

   a) In which city was this council held? (Acts 15:4) _____

   b) What burden did some in this council want to place on the Gentiles (non-Jews), according to Acts 15:5?

   _____

   c) What important decision was taken in this council by the other apostles and church leaders to support Paul and Barnabas in their opinion on this matter, according to our reading?

   _____

2. a) The Jerusalem church then chose two delegates to pass on officially this good news to their non-Jewish brethren. One of these delegates was Judas (not Judas Iscariot, of course); the other delegate was the man soon to join Paul on his **second** missionary journey.

   What was his name, according to our reading? _____

   b) What did the Jerusalem church send by the hand of these delegates? _____

3. So, accompanied by the two delegates, Paul and Barnabas set off happily on their return journey. On arrival, the delegates handed the encouraging letter to the church there. (See the map)

    a) Which city did they leave? _____

    b) At which city did they arrive to hand over the letter? _____

    c) What was the response of the church there to this letter?

    _____

4. a) It is important to remember that Silas originally came from the church that sent him out as their delegate. Which church was this?

        _____

    b) He was therefore, like Paul himself, obviously not a Gentile. What would his nationality have been?

        _____

5. A real unity now developed between the churches in Jerusalem and Antioch (in Syria) following the Jerusalem council. Here are some of the good things that happened as a result of this unity.

    A. It led to two churches of largely different nationalities encouraging and supporting each other as they did with this letter, rather than competing against each other (Acts 15:30).

    B. It made the Gentile Christians in Antioch glad (Acts 15:31).

    C. It made it easy for members of one congregation to visit another church and immediately to feel at home in the fellowship there as Silas and his fellow delegate did in Antioch (Acts 15:32–33).

    D. It made it easy to have a united project of outreach for the Lord as when Silas from Jerusalem joined Paul from Antioch on the second missionary journey (Acts 15:40–41).

    Which of these things are in evidence in the relationship between the churches in your area (especially in those of different denominations or ethnic or social backgrounds) and what could you do to help to improve on this?

    _____

    _____

6. We have considered four of the good things that happened as a result of the unity between the churches in Jerusalem and Antioch. All of these are important but, in the experience of the church in Antioch, one became clearly the most **far reaching**. Which one was this (A. B. C. or D. in Frame 5), and why?

    _____

    _____

    _____

7. So the unity between Christians led to a vast increase in evangelistic outreach to others. What did Jesus teach us about this in John 17:20–23 and what should we strive for in our own group as a result?

    _____

8.   Have a time of prayer asking that these things may be seen increasingly in the group as we advance in our studies.

9.   **Notices for Next Week**

a)   When you get home do the short test on this Introductory Study on page 92.

b)   There are usually two lessons (A and B) for home study. However, this week there is only one lesson, Lesson 1 (A and B together). This will give you a preview of Paul's second missionary journey, and the places and provinces he visited.

c)   Make sure you follow the **instructions** on Page 3 as you do the lessons.

d)   Please **review** this lesson before doing Test 1 (A and B), on pages 92 and 93 of this book. Then do Lesson 1C, but NOT the test for this lesson (this will be done AFTER the group meeting).

e)   Our next group meeting, to go over the tests and do Lesson 1C (Group Study) together, will be at:
(time) _____ (place) _____.

Lesson 1 (A and B)
Preview of the Second Journey
(Acts 16:11 to 18:17)

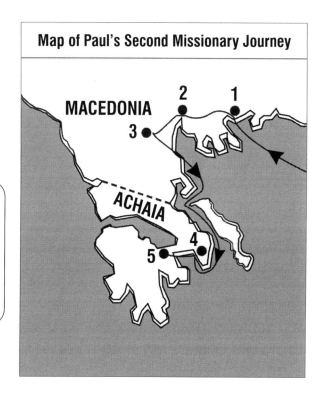

Map of Paul's Second Missionary Journey

*In our Introductory Group Study, we saw how the unity between the churches in Jerusalem and Antioch led to Silas (from Jerusalem) joining Paul (from Antioch) on Paul's **second** missionary journey, which we will be studying in this book. So here is a map of the main places they visited.*

1. From the map above we can see that of the two Roman provinces that Paul visited on his **second** missionary journey, the one to the north was called a) _____ and the one to the south was called b) _____.

2. On this second journey Paul visited **five** main towns, in the following order:

    a) _____ (Acts 16:12)

    b) _____ (Acts 17:1)

    c) _____ (Acts 17:10)

    d) _____ (Acts 17:16)

    e) _____ (Acts 18:1)

Answers

1. a) Macedonia
    b) Achaia

2. a) Philippi
    b) Thessalonica
    c) Berea
    d) Athens
    e) Corinth

3. **Exercise**

   Find these verses again in your N.I.V. Bible and draw a **red** ring around the name of each of these five towns. Also take note of the titles in your N.I.V. Bible. If you have a Bible that you don't want to mark with colors, you could mark it lightly with pencil instead and then erase it later. Unless you have some method of marking, you will be at a serious disadvantage in both the group discussions and in the Final Exam, as it is an integral part of the educational method in helping you to be able to find the right passages to share with others afterwards.

4. On the map on the previous page, these towns are **numbered** in the order in which Paul visited them. So we can see that:

   • In the **northern** province, called a) _____, Paul visited three towns:

   No.1 on the map, which is _____.

   No.2 on the map, which is _____.

   No.3 on the map, which is _____.

   • In the **southern** province of b) _____, Paul visited two towns:

   No.4 on the map, which is _____.

   No.5 on the map, which is _____.

   Memorize the position of each of these towns on the map.

5. All sorts of exciting things happened to Paul in these five towns. For the moment we are going to choose one event for each town. After reading thoughtfully each of the following references in your Bible, draw a line from its dot to the dot which marks the corresponding episode in the right hand column. Take note each time of the town where the event took place (using your marked Bible to find these).

1)	Acts 16:26 •	• a)	Jason's house is mobbed.
2)	Acts 17:5 •	• b)	Paul's vision of Jesus.
3)	Acts 17:11 •	• c)	Group Bible study.
4)	Acts 17:19 •	• d)	Earthquake.
5)	Acts 18:9 •	• e)	Invitation to preach in the Areopagus (city council).

6. Each of the following pictures illustrates one of the events given in Frame 5 above, but in the order in which they occurred. Using the titles in Frame 5, write these in the order in which they occurred, using the pictures as your guide.

Answers

4. a) Macedonia	4. b) Achaia	5. 1) — d)
No.1 Philippi	No.4 Athens	2) — a)
No.2 Thessalonica	No.5 Corinth	3) — c)
No.3 Berea		4) — e)
		5) — b)

Five "Key" Events of Paul's Second Journey
in their Order of Occurrence

Note: In all the pictures in this course, Paul's clothes are shaded with dots so that you can pick him out easily.

Events in order of occurrence:

Picture A   _____

Picture B   _____

Picture C   _____

Picture D   _____

Picture E   _____

Make sure you know these.

7.   Now review according to Instructions 4 and 5 on page 3. Repeat until absolutely sure of the names of all the towns and provinces and their position on the map; also our five chosen "key" events in the order in which they occurred. Once sure of them, do Test 1 (A and B) but **without** looking back to this lesson.

   Then do Lesson 1C.

Answers

6.   A   Earthquake
    B   Jason's house
    C   Group Bible Study
    D   Preaching in Areopagus
    E   Paul's vision of Jesus

Lesson 1C
Group Study
Paul's Second Journey and His Letters
(2 Peter 3:14–18)

1. Let's look again at the five "key" events of Paul's second missionary journey that we saw in Lesson 1 (A and B). Here are the references:

   1) Acts 16:25–26   3) Acts 17:11   5) Acts 18:9

   2) Acts 17:5   4) Acts 17:19

   Name the events again in the order in which they occurred and, using your marked Bibles, in each case give the town and province where they occurred.

   1) _____ _____ _____
   2) _____ _____ _____
   3) _____ _____ _____
   4) _____ _____ _____
   5) _____ _____ _____

2. **Review**

   Look back to the pictures in Lesson 1 (A and B) Frame 6 on page 9. Name the event illustrated by each picture and also the town and province where each occurred.

3. **Review**

   Look back to the map on the Title Page of Lesson 1 (A and B) and name the town marked by each number and also the "key" event which took place there.

4. Paul later wrote **letters** to **three** of these places that he visited on his **second** missionary journey.

   a) If necessary, look through your Bible to find them, looking only at the first page of each letter. There are 13 letters in all (the first is Romans and the last Philemon). Which of these were written to churches he set up on his **second** missionary journey?

   Name these **three** places. _____

   b) Two of these places received **two** of these letters each. Which were they? _____

   c) Which place received only **one** of these letters? _____

5. Now in this course, one of our most enjoyable and rewarding tasks will be to see how wonderfully Paul's letters throw new light on his life, and indeed vice versa. It is interesting, therefore, to see what the apostle Peter has to say about Paul's letters.

   Read 2 Peter 3:14–16. Find all the things that Peter says here that show his approval of Paul and of his teaching in his letters.

   _____

   _____

   _____

   _____

   🖉 **Note:** In verse 15, when Peter speaks of "our Lord's patience" he is referring to the "patience" by which the Lord delays his coming to allow more time for people to be saved (v.9).

6. Peter gives a glowing testimony both as to the great value of Paul's letters and as to their divine origin. However he also adds a warning note in vv.16–17. State in your own words what this warning is:

   _____

   _____

7. Peter urges us to be on our guard as we study Paul's letters. Read 2 Peter 3:17–18.

   What is it that we should constantly be on our guard

   a) **not** to do?   _____

   b) to **do**?   _____

8. **Discussion**

   How can we best avoid chasing fanciful and false interpretations when we study Paul's letters?

   How can we use the study and meditation of his letters to help us **grow** in the following two ways:

   • in grace (see what Paul says in 2 Timothy 2:1)?

   • in knowledge?

   What kind of knowledge is this? (See what Paul himself says in Philippians 3:10–11, and compare it with Philippians 3:7–8.)

9. Now let's pray together about the things we have learned in this study.

10. a) Please make sure you do Test 1C (on pages 93 and 94) **after** the Group Meeting, but **before** you start your next lesson. The tests on the Group Studies will be a great help to you when you come to your final review for the exam.

    b) Don't forget to do Lessons 2A and 2B (and their respective tests) for this week's home study. Then do Lesson 2C in preparation for the Group Meeting. As there are **three** lessons this week, make an **early** start.

Lesson 2A

Silas Joins Paul on His Second Journey: Lystra
(Acts 15:36–41)

Now let's go back to the start of Paul's second missionary journey, to see the events that led up to it. Look at Pictures A and B, before continuing.

Barnabas, let's revisit the church in Galatia that we set up on our first missionary journey.

Yes, and let's take John Mark again.

A

(Acts 15:36–37)

A.   Read Acts 15:36–41

B.   Now do the lesson (following the instructions on page 3).

1.   **Review**

You will remember how in Book 1 we learned that the province Paul visited on his **first** missionary journey was a) _____ (see Picture A above). Last week we saw that the main provinces he visited on the **second** journey were b) _____ and _____ (see map on page 7).

2.   However, when Paul started out from Antioch on this **second** journey he had no idea that God was going to lead him to Macedonia and Achaia. His strong desire at the time was rather to see again their many converts from his first missionary journey, in the province of Galatia.

Answers

1.   a) Galatia
     b) Macedonia and Achaia

So he suggested this to a) _____ (Picture A; Acts 15:36) who wanted to take
b) _____ _____ (Picture A; Acts 15:37) with them again.

3. "I don't think it is wise to take him" replied a) _____ (Picture B, below; Acts 15:38).
    "Remember how on our previous mission he b) _____ _____" (Picture B; Acts 15:38).

John Mark never!!
He turned back
before.
(Acts 15:38)

Paul, we must
take him and
give him another
chance!

B

4. Paul and Barnabas had such a sharp argument that they decided to p_____ c_____
    (Picture C 978-1-899049-57-8; Acts 15:39).

5. Barnabas took with him a) _____ (Picture C below; Acts 15:39) and Paul chose
    b) _____ (Picture C; Acts 15:40) who had been one of the delegates from the church in
    c) _____, (Review) and had carried the d) _____ (Acts 15:22–23) from the
    Council, and delivered it to the church in e) _____ (Acts 15:30).

Commissioned for second missionary journey

Paul and Silas, we commend you to the
care of the Lord's Grace. (Acts 15:40)

Come, John Mark, we'll go back to the
island of Cyprus. (Acts 15:39)

C

Answers

2. a) Barnabas
    b) John (Mark)

3. a) Paul
    b) deserted us
4. part company

5. a) John (Mark)
    b) Silas
    c) Jerusalem
    d) letter
    e) Antioch

6. So Barnabas returned to the island of a) _____ (Acts 15:39) accompanied by
    b) _____ _____ (Acts 15:39) who was his c) _____ (Col. 4:10). But the
    believers in Antioch commended d) _____ and e) _____ (Acts 15:40) to the Lord's
    f) _____ (Acts 15:40), after which they set off on the **second** missionary journey.

Return to Galatia

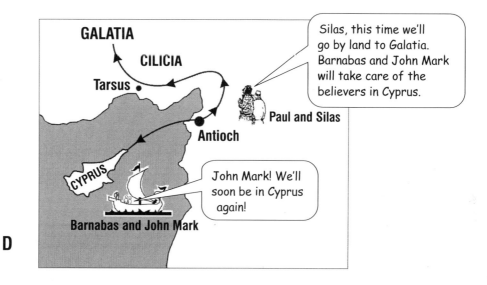

7. On the way to Galatia they passed through Cilicia (Acts 15:41); so Paul must surely have visited
    his home town of a) _____ (Picture D), whereas Barnabas (with his cousin John Mark)
    revisited the island where Barnabas had been born, which was called b) _____ (Acts 4:36).

8. **Exercise**

    Write above Acts 16:1 in your Bible the title "Second Missionary Journey – Acts 16:1 to 18:22".

9. **To Think and Pray About**

    On the first missionary journey Mark's deserting led to an unhappy split between Paul and
    Barnabas (Acts 15:36–40). However, the break with Paul led to a new relationship with Peter
    from whom Mark got fresh material to write his gospel. The split was wrong, but God overruled
    it for good.

    How does this illustrate what Paul says in Romans 8:28 and what experience do you have of
    this truth?

10. Now review until perfect and then do Test 2A (at home) before going on to Lesson 2B.

Answers

6. a) Cyprus	7. a) Tarsus
b) John Mark	b) Cyprus
c) cousin	
d) Paul	
e) Silas	
f) grace	

Lesson 2B
Timothy Joins Paul in Lystra
(Acts 16:1–5)

1. Paul was now well on his way with his a) _____ missionary journey (see your marked Bible). From Tarsus, in the province of Cilicia, he traveled on, with his companion b) _____, until they came to the city of c) _____ (Picture; Acts 16:1) in Galatia. Here he met again his beloved young friend called d) _____ (Picture; Acts 16:1) who had been converted on his e) _____ missionary journey (Review) along with two other members of his family, namely his f) _____ called g) _____ (2 Tim. 1:5), and his h) _____ called i) _____ (2 Tim. 1:5).

2. Notice in 1. f), g), h) and i) above how the letter Paul wrote years later to _____ throws so much light on what happened on his missionary journeys.

3. Timothy's parents were of different nationalities (Acts 16:1); his mother was a) _____ and his father was a b) _____.

4. Following his conversion during Paul's first missionary journey, Timothy had been completely transformed by Christ; we know this because all the believers in _____ (Acts 16:2) and Iconium testified to the change.

Answers

1. a) second	1. f) grandmother	3. a) Jewish
b) Silas	g) Lois	b) Greek
c) Lystra	h) mother	4. Lystra
d) Timothy	i) Eunice	
e) first	2. Timothy	

5. Now Timothy decided to accept Paul's invitation to a) _____ (Acts 16:3) with him. But before he could do this Paul decided to b) _____ him (Acts 16:3).

6. This may seem strange, because previously Paul had refused to circumcise _____ (Gal. 2:3).

7. The difference between Timothy and Titus is, however, that Titus was a pure-blooded a) _____ (Gal. 2:3) (both his parents were non-Jews) whereas in Timothy's case only one of his parents was a Greek, that was his b) _____ (Acts 16:3).

8. Now according to **Jewish** ideas, in mixed marriages between a Jew and a non-Jew the children take the **mother's** nationality, so in their eyes Timothy was a a) _____. As Paul always tried to witness in the Jewish synagogues, this would have been impossible if Timothy, his companion, had not been b) _____.

9. So remember, Paul refused to circumcise a) _____ because he was a b) _____; he did circumcise c) _____ because in the eyes of the Jews he was a d) _____, because his e) _____ was Jewish, and all the Jews knew his father was a f) _____. So he circumcised Timothy in consideration for the g) _____.

10. As the missionary party moved around Galatia they delivered the contents of the letter that the Council in a) _____ (Acts 16:4) had sent out by the hand of their delegate b) _____ (Acts 15:22–23), and urged them to obey it.

11. This had a double beneficial effect upon the churches:

    They were a) _____ in the b) _____ (Acts 16:5). They c) _____ daily in d) _____ (Acts 16:5).

12. The missionary party also had grown; they were now three in number, that is, a) _____, b) _____ and their new young companion c) _____.

13. **To Think About**

    Read what Paul wrote about Timothy more than ten years later, in Philippians 2:19–22.

    a) What words in this passage show Paul's appreciation and gratitude toward his young companion, Timothy?

    b) Are you like Timothy, one who "takes a genuine interest" in other people (v.20), one who has "proved himself"?

    c) Are you like Timothy, "serving with others in the work of the Gospel" (v.22)?

    Who will help you to keep going, however hard the way may be? Pray for this help now.

14. Now review well, and do Test 2B. Then do Lesson 2C for the Group Meeting.

Answers

5. a) go	9. a) Titus	10. a) Jerusalem b) Silas
b) circumcise	b) Greek	11. a) strengthened
6. Titus	c) Timothy	b) faith
7. a) Greek	d) Jew	c) grew
b) father	e) mother	d) numbers
8. a) Jew	f) Greek	12. a) Paul
b) circumcised	g) Jews	b) Silas
		c) Timothy

Lesson 2C
Group Study

Paul's Letters to Timothy: On-the-Job Training
(1 and 2 Timothy)

In our last lesson we saw how Timothy joined the missionary team with Paul and Silas. In the New Testament we have two letters Paul wrote to Timothy. Although he wrote these years later, nevertheless they teach us a lot about Timothy, so find them now.
They will teach us about three things:
* A. The MAN Paul trained (Timothy).*
* B. The MATERIAL Paul used to train him.*
* C. The METHOD he used to train him.*

A. The MAN Paul trained (Timothy)

1. Where was Timothy when Paul wrote to him? (See 1 Timothy 1:3) _____

2. **Exercise**

    Draw a **red** ring around the word "Ephesus" in your Bible in 1 Timothy 1:3 and 2 Timothy 1:18 to remind you that Paul wrote this first letter when Timothy was in Ephesus, and probably the second letter too.

3. What can we learn about Timothy's family background from these letters? Read 2 Timothy 1:5 and 3:15. Compare with Acts 16:1.

    _____

    _____

    _____

4. a) What more can we learn about Timothy from the way Paul refers to him in 1 Timothy 1:2 and 2 Timothy 1:2? (Optional references: 1 Cor. 4:17; Phil. 2:22; 1 Tim. 1:18a; 2 Tim. 2:1a.)

        _____

        _____

    b) What does this teach us about the time and place where Timothy and his family became Christians?

        _____

        _____

        _____

5. **Exercise**

Write "Tim." in the margin of the verses we have looked at, which give us background material on Timothy, so that you can find them again easily. These are 2 Timothy 1:2; 1:5; and 3:15.

6. What further interesting personal details about Timothy can we learn from each of the following verses? Remember Paul's warnings to Timothy probably indicate a potential weakness in his character.

✎ **Note:** As you read and discuss each verse, write "Tim." in the margin.

a) 1 Tim. 4:12 _____

b) 1 Tim. 5:23 _____

c) 2 Tim. 1:4 _____

d) 2 Tim. 1:7 _____

e) 2 Tim. 1:8; 2:3–7 _____

f) 2 Tim. 2:22 (compare 1 Tim. 5:2b) _____

_____

B. The MATERIAL Paul used to train Timothy

C. The METHOD Paul used to train him

7. This then was the young man from Lystra in Galatia whom Paul wanted to join his missionary team in order to train him for ministry. Now read 2 Timothy 3:10–11.

a) Let's look at the **material** Paul used (i.e. the things he taught). What marvelous and exciting things did Paul teach Timothy in his training?

Discuss which of these were especially suitable for a person with the characteristics that we have seen Timothy had, and why?

Are any of them especially applicable to you?

_____

_____

_____

b) Now discuss the **method** that Paul used to teach this material, according to verse 11.

_____

_____

_____

8. **Exercise**

Write "Mat." in the margin of 2 Timothy 3:10 (for **Material**) and

"Meth." in the margin of 2 Timothy 3:11 (for **Method**)

9. As a basis for everything, Paul's students were taught to trust the Bible, and to **know how to use it effectively**. Read 2 Timothy 3:16.

    a) What view of the Bible were they taught?

    _____

    b) In which four ways were they especially taught to use the Bible?

    _____

    _____

    _____

    _____

    🖉 **Note**: This is why we are marking our Bibles: not only for our own benefit, but also so that we can **find** the teaching again, and **use it** to help others.

10. Read 2 Timothy 3:17.

    a) What would a "thoroughly equipped" person in Paul's training course be able to do?

    _____

    b) How would you describe this kind of training course?

    _____

11. So how can we become "thoroughly equipped" in this kind of ministry? Read 1 Timothy 4:7b. (Write "Meth." in the margin)

    _____

    _____

12. Read 1 Timothy 4:8. (Write "Meth." in the margin)

    The word Paul uses here for "physical training" is the one from which we get our word "gym" and "gymnasium". So what must we do if we want our own training course to be a success?

    Compare with 1 Timothy 4:10, 15 and 16 (Write "Meth." by each of these)

    _____

    _____

    _____

    _____

    _____

    _____

    _____

    _____

13. What was the ultimate objective of Paul's training course, which made it such a dynamic and explosive thing? It is clearly set forth in 2 Timothy 2:2, which is also the motto of SEAN: *"Be qualified (able/ equipped) to teach others"*. (Write "Meth." in the margin)

_____

_____

_____

14. Sometimes people look down on "on-the-job" training, forgetting that both Jesus and Paul used this method with the most wonderful results. As we have seen, Paul felt such people were "thoroughly equipped". (2 Tim. 3:17)

    What high office did Timothy come to exercise as a result of this kind of training? Read and compare 1 Timothy 1:3 with 2 Timothy 2:2 and 1 Timothy 5:22.

_____

_____

15. Paul's letters to Timothy are just packed with the things Paul wanted to teach him in his on-the-job training while Timothy was in Ephesus; training others to train others!

    Below is a list of some of the more important of these. If you have time, choose one or two of them and discuss them now. If not, just glance through them and look at them in more detail when you get home.

> **Subjects taught by Paul while training Timothy:**
>
> a) How to deal with false doctrine. (1 Tim. 1:3–10; 4:1–5; 6:3–5)
>
> b) Counsel on praying in the church. (1 Tim. 2:1–4, 8)
>
> c) Qualities required for church leaders. (1 Tim. 3:1–13)
>
> d) How to cope with the generation gap. (1 Tim. 5:1–2)
>
> e) Care of widows in the church. (1 Tim. 5:3–16)
>
> f) Treatment of church elders. (1 Tim. 5:17–22)
>
> g) Advice on social problems. (1 Tim. 6:1–2)
>
> h) Lifestyle in the church:
>
> • for women. (1 Tim. 2:9–10)
>
> • for men. (1 Tim. 6:5b–10)
>
> i) General advice to pastors, young and old (1 Tim. 4:6–16; 2 Tim. 2:1–7; 2 Tim. 2:14 to 4:5)
>
> j) Doctrine (1 Tim. 1:17; 2:5–6; 6:13–16; 2 Tim. 1:9–10; 2:11–13)

16. Let's **pray together**, asking for real opportunities to **practice** the wonderful truths we have learned from his word today (e.g. **practice** loving people and God better, growing in faith, in endurance under difficulty, in purpose, in good conduct, etc.)

17. For **next week's Group Meeting**, please do the following at home:

    a) Test 2C for this lesson.

    b) Lessons 3A and 3B and their tests; they tell how a **fourth** member joined the missionary team. We will also learn more about Timothy.

    c) Lesson 3C in preparation for the Group Meeting.

Lesson 3A

Luke Joins Paul in Troas

(Acts 16:6–10)

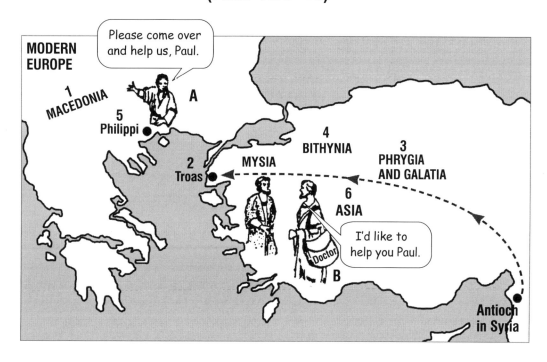

Important:

A. Read Acts 16:6–10

B. Look at the map above and follow the arrows marking Paul's route.
(The names of towns are in small letters, those of regions, in capitals.)

C. Do the lesson.

1. On leaving the region of Phrygia and Galatia, marked on the above map by the number a) ____, Paul wanted to preach the word in the important province of b) _____ (Acts 16:6), marked on the map by the number c) _____. However, when he tried to go there, he was prevented from doing so by the d) _____ _____ (Acts 16:6).

2. When they reached the border of Mysia they tried to go into a) _____ (Acts 16:7), marked on the map by the number b) _____ but once again they were stopped from doing so by the c) _____ of _____ (Acts 16:7).

Answers

1. a) 3
   b) Asia
   c) 6
   d) Holy Spirit

2. a) Bithynia
   b) 4
   c) Spirit of Jesus

3. So leaving Asia on their a) _____ hand side (see map), and Bithynia on the b) _____ hand side (map), they went straight ahead until they came to the coastal town of c) _____ (Acts 16:8), marked on the map by the number d) _____.

4. This is an excellent example of how Paul was guided by the Holy Spirit. Of the four examples given below, the right one that Paul used here to find God's guidance, is Letter _____.

   A. Putting a pin haphazardly on a verse in the Bible, hoping God will direct your hand to the one that has his guidance for you.

   B. Prayerfully "testing the doors", confident that God will shut the wrong doors and open the right one.

   C. Making your mind a blank and hoping the first thing that comes into it will be God's guidance.

   D. Not doing anything until God writes his plan across the sky.

5. Of course God shut the door on a) _____ and Bithynia at this time because he had something much better prepared for Paul as he continued on to the coastal town of b) _____.

6. In this town he met up with the person who would be the author of the Acts of the Apostles. This man also wrote the third Gospel, so we know that his name was a) _____. By profession he was a b) _____ (Col. 4:14). He was also the only writer in the New Testament who was not a Jew, but a c) _____.

7. On his first missionary journey, while in Galatia, Paul fell a) _____ (Gal. 4:13). We learned last week that Timothy was also often b) _____ (1 Tim. 5:23). So it must have been a great comfort to Paul to have Luke join him in the town of c) _____, because he was a d) _____.

8. Luke, the author of Acts, was a most humble man and never refers to himself directly in his books. How then do we know that he joined the party in a) _____? We know because when he is **not** present he says **"they"** did this and **"they"** did that, but when he **is** present he gives this fact away by saying **"we"** did this, and **"we"** did that. The use of the word "we" shows that b) _____ was present.

9. Now read Acts 16:6 carefully. According to what it says here we can see that Luke [was/was not] present (Underline the correct answer).

10. When they had arrived in a) _____ (Acts 16:8) we read *"After Paul had seen the vision,* b) _____ *(Acts 16:10) got ready at once to leave for Macedonia, concluding that God had called* c) _____ *(Acts 16:10) (not 'them') to preach the gospel to them."* So now we can see that d) _____, who was writing this account, had joined the group in the town of e) _____.

Answers

3. a) left	5. a) Asia	7. a) ill	9. was not
b) right	b) Troas	b) ill	10. a) Troas
c) Troas	6. a) Luke	c) Troas	b) we
d) 2	b) doctor	d) doctor	c) us
4. B.	c) Gentile	8. a) Troas	d) Luke
		b) Luke (or "he")	e) Troas

11. **Exercise**

    With red pencil

    a) make a ring in your Bible around the words:

    "Troas" in Acts 16:8,

    "We" and **"us"** in Acts 16:10.

    b) write "Luke" in the margin to remind you that it was in Troas that Luke joined the team, and that we know this because the **"we"** passages start here.

12. **To Think About**

    1) What danger does Paul warn us against in Romans 12:3?

       a) How did the Pharisees fall into this trap in Luke 11:43?

       b) Even the disciples sometimes fell into this trap. How? (Luke 22:24)

    2) a) How do we know that Luke overcame this temptation to an enormous degree?

       b) What must we do if we are ever going to overcome this temptation? (Read Matt. 18:4)

       c) What does the Lord promise to people who are humble like Luke? (Read James 4:10)

    3) How do you stand on this matter? What are the areas in your life where you should work and pray for an improvement?

13. So the **first** important reason why God brought Paul to Troas was so that he would meet up there with a) _____ who was by profession a b) _____ and who would now join Paul's team.

14. The **second** important reason was because God wanted Paul to cross the sea and preach the Good News in a) _____ (Acts 16:10). Now God made this clear to Paul in Troas when Paul saw in a b) _____ (Acts 16:9) a man begging him to come over and help them. This man was a c) _____ (Acts 16:9). All this took place during the d) _____ (Acts 16:9). As a result they all set out for e) _____ (Acts 16:10), marked on the map on the Title Page of this lesson by the number f) ____.

15. This was a very big step forward because in crossing the sea to a) _____ they were carrying the gospel for the first time into the continent that today is called b) _____ (map).

16. On the map on the Title Page of this lesson, the man that represents Luke joining Paul as a new companion, is the one marked by Letter a) ____.

    The man on the map that represents the Macedonian calling Paul to a new destination, is the one marked by Letter b) ____.

Answers

13. a) Luke
    b) doctor

14. a) Macedonia
    b) vision
    c) Macedonian
    d) night
    e) Macedonia
    f) 1

15. a) Macedonia
    b) Europe
16. a) B
    b) A

17. It is important to remember that God guided Paul to the coastal town of **Troas** for **two** reasons:

    He got a new companion there, a) _____ the b) _____.

    There, he was called to a new continent; this was the continent we call today c) _____.
    The province where they first arrived was d) _____.

18. So the team set sail from Troas to Macedonia. They were now four in number; that is a) _____,
    b) _____, c) _____ and d) _____.

19. Now review and do Test 3A. Then go on to Lesson 3B.

✎ **Note:** In your review, don't try to memorize the numbers and letters that mark places on the map but find them again on the map each time you review, until you are sure you can recognize all their positions, and name the places referred to.

Answers

17. a) Luke
    b) doctor
    c) Europe
    d) Macedonia

18. a) Paul
    b) Silas
    c) Timothy
    d) Luke

Lesson 3B
Paul Enters Macedonia: Philippi
(Acts 16:11–40)

We are going to read the story of Paul's stay in Philippi in four parts, each of which deals with a person who played a significant role in Paul's ministry in that city. The following pictures show these four people. Look at them now before starting the lesson.

A

Yes Luke, praise God!

Look, Silas and Timothy, all Lydia's household also believe.

Lydia, do you confess the name of Jesus as your Messiah?

Yes, the Lord has opened my heart.

DOCTOR

A. Lydia

Read Acts 16:11–15 and compare with Picture A on the Title Page of this lesson.

1. To reach Neapolis in Macedonia from Troas only took them a) _____ days (Acts 16:11), a journey which on another occasion in the opposite direction took them a good b) _____ days (Acts 20:6). So clearly the Lord sent favorable winds on this vital occasion.

2. From Neapolis they went straight to a) _____ (Acts 16:12), marked on the map on the Title Page of Lesson 1 (A and B) by the number b) _____. This was the first town where Paul stayed and ministered in the province of c) _____ (see map).

3. Philippi was very different from the other towns they had visited so far, because it was completely dominated by the Romans. It was a military center and so it was full of a) _____ soldiers. Luke called it a Roman b) _____ (Acts 16:12).

4. Also Paul could not follow his usual custom, because in Philippi there was no Jewish
    a) _____. Instead, the four missionaries, b) _____, c) _____,
    d) _____ and e) _____, walked out through the city gate and down to the place where people used to gather for f) _____ (Acts 16:13) in the open air by the side of the g) _____ (Acts 16:13).

5. Here they found a little group of a) _____ (Acts 16:13) and, having introduced themselves, Paul told them about Jesus. Immediately the Lord opened the heart of a woman called b) _____ (Acts 16:14), who accepted all Paul said. She ran a business in Philippi selling c) _____ (Acts 16:14) and appears to have been quite wealthy.

6. Immediately Lydia was a) _____ (Acts 16:15), and so were all the members of her b) _____ (Acts 16:15).

7. She now invited Paul and his colleagues to stay in her house. And so while they remained in a) _____ they all stayed in the house of b) _____.

B. A Girl with an Evil Spirit

Read Acts 16:16–24 and compare with Picture B, on page 28.

8. Every day the team went down to the riverside to pray and to teach the new Christians. Timothy, of course, would have listened and watched Paul in action; it was a vital part of his training. One day, they were met by a a) _____ _____ (Acts 16:16), who was possessed by a b) _____ and who earned a lot of money for her owners by c) _____ _____. She kept shouting after Paul; this went on for d) _____ _____ (Acts 16:18). Paul was so upset that he ordered the evil spirit to e) _____ _____ of her.

Answers

1. a) 2
    b) 5
2. a) Philippi
    b) 1
    c) Macedonia
3. a) Roman
    b) colony
	4. a) synagogue
	    b) Paul
	    c) Silas
	    d) Timothy
	    e) Luke
	    f) prayer
	    g) river
		5. a) women
		    b) Lydia
		    c) purple cloth
		6. a) baptized
		    b) household
		7. a) Philippi
		    b) Lydia
			8. a) slave girl
			    b) spirit
			    c) fortune telling
			    d) many days
			    e) come out

9. The girl's owners were enraged to lose this easy way of making money. So they dragged a) _____ and b) _____ (Acts 16:19) before the b) _____ (Acts 16:19) in the c) _____ _____.

10. Philippi was a Roman garrison city and the authorities accused them of being a) _____ (Acts 16:20) who were breaking the b) _____ law (Acts 16:21). So, without waiting for proof, they condemned them to a double punishment: first, to be c) _____ and d) _____ (Acts 16:22), and secondly, to be e) _____ _____ _____ (Acts 16:23–24).

C. The Philippian Jailer

Read Acts 16:25–34 and compare with Picture C, on page 28.

11. But even though the jailer threw them into the inner cell and put them in the stocks, Paul and Silas refused to lose heart. Although in terrible pain, they began both to a) _____ (Acts 16:25) and even to b) _____ hymns, so that all the c) _____ heard them. What a witness!

12. Suddenly God sent a great a) _____ (Acts 16:26), so powerful that the jailer thought all the prisoners had escaped and so decided to b) _____ _____ (Acts 16:27), because by Roman law he would have been completely disgraced.

13. However Paul shouted to him not to a) _____ himself (Acts 16:28) because they were all there, and then told him about Jesus. The result was that the b) _____ (Acts 16:30, 34) was converted.

14. He took Paul and Silas into his house and washed their wounds. They preached to all in his house. Then the jailer was a) _____ (Acts 16:33) with all his b) _____ (Acts 16:33).

15. So it is interesting to note that in the case of the two individuals that Paul tells us were converted in Philippi, that is a) _____ (Acts 16:14) and the b) _____ (Acts 16:29–31), both were immediately c) _____ (Acts 16:15 and 33) and both took this step with all their d) _____ (Acts 16:15 and 33).

D. Luke stays on in Philippi, as Paul says farewell

Read Acts 16:35–40 and compare with Picture D, on page 28.

16. Now look back to the five pictures on page 9. The one that represents Paul's time in Philippi is Picture _____.

Answers

9 . a) Paul	10. d) beaten	12. a) earthquake	15. a) Lydia
b) Silas	e) thrown into prison	b) kill himself	b) jailer
c) authorities	11. a) pray	13. a) harm	c) baptized
d) market place	b) sing	b) jailer	d) household or family
10. a) Jews	c) prisoners	14. a) baptized	16. A
b) Roman		b) family	
c) stripped			

17. The next morning the Roman authorities sent police officers with an order to release Paul and Silas. But Paul refused to go, on the grounds that he was a _____ _____ (Acts 16:37).

18. In the days of the Roman Empire, to have "Roman citizenship" was a tremendous advantage. Anybody, whatever his nationality, if he had this, could count on the protection of the military might of Rome throughout the whole empire. There were various ways in which a person could receive such an honor: as a reward for special services, or by buying it with a large sum of money. Sometimes it could be passed on from father to son. Some time later Paul was asked if he was a a) _____ _____ (Acts 22:27) to which he replied, b) "_____". The Roman commander, who asked him the question, had had to buy his with a large amount of c) _____ (Acts 22:28). Paul explained that in his case he had received it by d) _____ (Acts 22:28); that is, it had been passed down to him from his e) _____ .

19. In sending his reply to the Roman officials, Paul reminded them that they had condemned Silas and him to be a) _____ (Acts 16:37) and thrown into b) _____ (Acts 16:37) without a proper trial or any evidence of guilt. The officials were horrified when they heard that Paul was a c) _____ _____ (v.38).

20. So the officials had to come personally to apologize to them and ask them to leave the city of a) _____ . After returning to the house of b) _____ they decided to do this to avoid causing more disturbance, and they traveled on through various places until they came to c) _____ (Acts 17:1), their next place for ministry.

21. Remember, four members of the team arrived in Philippi; they were a) _____, b) _____, c) _____ and d) _____. However only two of them left there, that is e) _____ and f) _____ (Acts 17:1, 4). This means that g) _____ and h) _____ stayed on in Philippi to help the new church there.

22. Of the two who stayed on in Philippi, one followed Paul and Silas fairly soon after, catching up with them in Berea. This was _____ (Acts 17:14).

23. The last member of the team to leave Philippi, therefore, was a) _____. He stayed on there all the time that Paul was away and indeed until Paul revisited Philippi on his **third** missionary journey. We know this because from now onwards, in describing what Paul and the others did, he no longer writes "we" did this and "we" did that, but instead says *"on arriving there* b) _____ *went to the Jewish synagogue"* (Acts 17:10).

24. Indeed it is only when Paul at last got back to Macedonia on his **third** missionary journey that Luke suddenly starts to write: "_____ (Acts 20:6) *sailed from Philippi."* What a wonderful example of Luke's amazing truthfulness and accuracy! Try to remember this.

Answers

17. Roman citizen
18. a) Roman citizen
    b) Yes
    c) money
    d) birth
    e) father

19. a) beaten
    b) prison
    c) Roman citizen
20. a) Philippi
    b) Lydia
    c) Thessalonica

21. a) Paul
    b) Silas
    c) Timothy
    d) Luke
    e) Paul
    f) Silas

21. g) Timothy
    h) Luke
22. Timothy
23. a) Luke
    b) they
24. we

25. **Exercise**

   A. Under Acts 16:40 write **"Luke Stays On"** to remind you that here the "we" passages end.

   B. With red pencil

   a) make a ring in your Bible around the words:

   • **"we"** twice in Acts 20:6,

   • **"from Philippi"** in Acts 20:6.

   b) write: **"Luke Again"** under Acts 20:6 to remind you that it was in **Philippi** that Paul met up again with Luke who had been there guiding the church ever since Paul left, as we see in Acts 16:40.

26. **To Think About**

   Luke

   a) Scholars think that Paul was about **50 years old** when he left Luke in Philippi (Acts 16:40). He must have been **about 56** when he finally got back to Philippi in Acts 20:6 and met up again with Luke.

   How long does it seem that Luke was in Philippi, helping the church in Paul's absence?

   b) From then on Luke became Paul's constant traveling companion staying by his side until, at **about 67**, Paul was executed in Rome. Just before Paul was executed, what did he say about Luke? (2 Tim. 4:11)

   c) In what way was Luke a good example of 1 Corinthians 15:58?

   d) What can you learn from Luke's example, for your own life? (See Gal. 6:9)

27. Look at the four pictures at the beginning of this lesson and write the letter of the picture that matches each of the people below:

   a) The Philippian jailer.   Picture _____

   b) Lydia.   Picture _____

   c) Luke.   Picture _____

   d) The girl with an evil spirit.   Picture _____

28. Remember to review, and do Test 3B. Then do Lesson 3C.

Answers

27. a) C
    b) A
    c) D
    d) B

Lesson 3C
Group Study

Paul's Letter to the Philippians
(Philippians)

Introduction

1. We are now going to study the letter Paul wrote to the Philippian church. From this we shall see that it became Paul's strongest supporting church. Where was Paul when he wrote this letter? Read Philippians 1:7.

   _____

2. a) Who played a part in writing the letter, probably as Paul's secretary? (See Phil. 1:1)

   _____

   b) Who does it seem took the letter to Philippi? (Phil. 2:25 gives us a clue)

   _____

3. Read Philippians 2:19–24. When we remember that Paul must have written these words around 10 years after founding the church in Philippi we can see how effective and long lasting his training of Timothy had been. Review briefly what we have already seen, by comparing and contrasting these two young helpers that Paul had.

   • Timothy (Phil. 2:19–24)
   • John Mark (Acts 15:37-39; Col. 4:10; 2 Tim. 4:11)

   a) What did they have in common?

   _____

   _____

   b) What differences were there between them?

   _____

   _____

   _____

   c) Who restored John Mark back into service? (Acts 15:38-39) _____

   d) What does this teach us about the blessing of being given a second chance?

   _____

   _____

   _____

But Paul's letter to the Philippians not only tells us lots of good things about Timothy, it also does the same about the church in Philippi. Truly this church was one of Paul's top success stories; it certainly became his strongest supporting church. We'll look at this under two headings.

A. "WHEN" the Philippians supported Paul

B. "HOW" the Philippians supported Paul

A. WHEN the Philippians supported Paul

4. Read Philippians 1:4–5.

    a) What had the Philippian church done for Paul?

    _____

    b) For how long?

    _____

    _____

5. How had they helped Paul's ministry literally on the very **first** day? Read again Acts 16:15; compare also with Acts 16:33–34.

    _____

    _____

6. a) On what other occasion had the Philippians helped Paul in his work of the gospel, from the very earliest days? Read Philippians 4:16.

    _____

    b) How soon after the church in Philippi had been established did this happen?

    _____

    _____

    c) Was it a "one-off" case of help?

    _____

    _____

    _____

7. You will remember that on leaving Macedonia, Paul then went on to Athens and Corinth, in Achaia.

    a) And what did the Philippian church do for Paul then? Read Philippians 4:14–15.

    _____

b) When Paul wrote to the Corinthians, he reminded them that he received help of money when he worked among them. Where did the people who brought this help come from? (2 Cor. 11:9)

_____

c) What did the other churches in Macedonia (Thessalonica and Berea) do for Paul when he was in Achaia? (Phil. 4:15)

_____

8. And now, nearly ten years later, Paul is writing to thank the Philippians once again.

a) In what special need was Paul at the time, that led to them sending help once again? (Phil. 1:7)

_____

b) At what other times had they helped Paul? Read Philippians 1:7.

_____

9. Clearly the support of the Philippians for Paul had been most constant. Had there been any time when they had **not** sent help directly to Paul? Read Philippians 4:10–11.

_____

10. Did this mean they had stopped giving to God's work? Certainly not! Read 2 Corinthians 8:1–2, written to Corinth in Achaia.

a) To which churches is Paul here referring as giving churches?

_____

b) To whom were they giving on this occasion? Read Romans 15:25–26.

_____

11. We will see that Paul organized this collection for the poor in Jerusalem during his **third** missionary journey, and it was to him very important. We shall return to this again in Book 3. If you have time, (or leave for home study) read 1 Corinthians 16:1–2 and Romans 15:26 where Paul shows how the churches in **Galatia**, **Macedonia** and **Achaia** (i.e. **all** the churches he had founded on his **first** and **second** missionary journeys) joined in this aid fund for the poor in Jerusalem.

12. So here we get a glimpse of Paul's great love and concern for those in special need, and of his great organizing ability.

To get an insight into how Paul used the generosity of the churches in Macedonia (especially Philippi) to encourage Corinth (in Achaia) also to participate fully, read aloud the following passages (but without comment for they speak for themselves):

- 2 Corinthians 8:8 (Here he is talking about the churches in Macedonia, and especially Philippi)
- 2 Corinthians 9:1–5

  Make a mental note that these two chapters, 8 and 9 of 2 Corinthians, are all about giving and the aid fund for the poor in Judea.

13. **Summary**

Go over the following passages again, naming the five occasions that we have just studied **"WHEN"** the Philippians supported Paul.

✎ **Note:** As you read each verse, write "Gift 1", "Gift 2", etc. by its side in your Bible to help you to find them again.

GIFT 1 (Phil. 1:5)

_____

GIFT 2 (Phil. 4:16)

_____

GIFT 3 (Phil. 4:15 and 2 Cor. 11:9)

_____

GIFT 4 (2 Cor. 8:1–4)

_____

GIFT 5 (Phil. 4:18)

_____

B. HOW the Philippians supported Paul

14. a) What was the secret behind such generosity in Philippi? Read 2 Corinthians 8:5.

_____

b) So how did they approach the whole matter of giving? Read 2 Corinthians 8:4.

_____

15. But as we have seen, the underlying principle that led to such generosity in Philippi was that they had first given **themselves** in unqualified surrender to the Lord and to his service.

Now Paul gives us a simply wonderful example of this in his letter to the Philippians.

a) What was the name of the Philippian Christian who had brought their gifts for Paul in prison all the way from Philippi to Rome?

Read Philippians 4:18.   _____

b) But this dear Christian friend did much more than just carry and deliver the gifts to Paul. What more did he do?

Read Philippians 2:25–30 listing the main points.

_____

_____

_____

_____

16. This was the kind of support that Paul constantly received from the church in Philippi. Remember that this church was made up of many people like Epaphroditus.

    a) Who were some of these lovely Christians that we saw in Lesson 3B?

    _____

    b) In what way were they like Epaphroditus, according to 2 Corinthians 8:5?

    _____

    _____

17. How does Paul describe the kind of sacrifice made by Lydia, the jailer, their families and Epaphroditus, etc. in Philippians 4:18?

    _____

18. Now let's sum up these points on **HOW** the Philippians supported Paul in his work for Christ, and what this teaches us. List all the different ways in which they did this, that you can remember from this study.

    _____

    _____

    _____

    _____

    _____

    _____

    _____

    _____

    _____

    _____

    _____

    _____

    _____

    _____

19. Please will someone read 2 Corinthians 8:9 and Romans 12:1, and then we will have a time of open prayer, based on its challenge.

20. For **next week's Group Meeting,** please do the following at home:

    a) Test 3C for this lesson.

    b) Lessons 4A and 4B which tell us how Paul ministered in the next town, Thessalonica. Review well and do Tests 4A and 4B.

    c) Lesson 4C in preparation for the Group Meeting.

Lesson 4A
Paul in Thessalonica: The Synagogue
(Acts 17:1–4)

A.   Read Acts 17:1–4. (Put a marker on this place in your Bible.)

B.   Look carefully at this map and use it throughout this lesson.

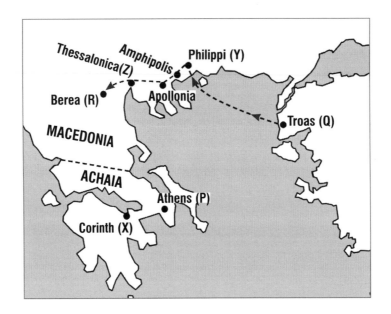

C.   Now do the lesson, especially noting how Paul's letters to the Thessalonians agree with Luke's account in the Acts and fill in many important details for us.

1.   We learned in the last lesson that when the missionaries left a) _____ (see Letter Q on map) and arrived in b) _____ (see Letter Y on map) there were four of them in the team, **Paul**, **Silas**, **Timothy** and **Luke**.

2.   However only **two** of these left Philippi for Thessalonica; these were a) _____ and b) _____ (Acts 17:1, 4).

3.   This meant that the other two, a) _____ and b) _____, were left in Philippi to look after the new converts there.

Answers		

1. a) Troas
   b) Philippi
	2. a) Paul
	   b) Silas
		3. a) Timothy
		   b) Luke

4. The fact that the "we" passage, which tells us that the author of Acts is in the party, ends in Philippi (Acts 16) and does not start again until Acts 20:6 also suggests that the author of Acts, who is a) _____, wasn't in the party all this time but remained behind in b) _____ to guide the new converts there.

5. So having passed through Amphipolis and Apollonia, Paul, accompanied by a) _____ (Acts 17:1, 4), arrived in b) _____ (Letter Z on map).

6. From Philippi to Thessalonica was a journey of about a) _____ miles (see milestone), along the famous Roman road called the b) _____ _____ (see milestone). Like Philippi, Thessalonica was in the province of c) _____ (see the map on the previous page).

7. Paul and Silas went to the Jewish a) _____ (Acts 17:2–3) each Sabbath (Saturday), this over a period of b) _____ weeks.

8. Here Paul taught about the suffering (death) and resurrection of Jesus, showing from the a) _____ (Acts 17:2–3) that he was indeed the long awaited b) _____.

9. Now let's fill in the background by looking at the letter Paul later wrote to the Thessalonians. He wrote this letter from the city of _____ (Letter X on the map).

10. Read 1 Thessalonians 2:2. In this verse Paul tells the Thessalonians that to preach to them needed a lot of courage because they had arrived in a state of complete physical exhaustion, having a) _____ and been treated b) _____ in c) _____, just before traveling on to d) _____.

🖉 **Note:** Make sure you can find Paul's two letters to the Thessalonians in future: they come after Colossians and before 1 Timothy.

11. Remember Paul tells us about his arrival in Thessalonica from Philippi in his a) _____ letter to the Thessalonians (see Frame 10 above) which agrees exactly with the account in Acts which was written by b) _____.

12. Remember, too, that Paul wrote his two letters to the Thessalonians when he got to the city of _____ (Review).

13. Not only were some of the Jews convinced by Paul's message but also some of the leading women and a large group of _____ (Acts 17:4) who used to go to the synagogue to worship the true God.

Answers

4. a) Luke	7. a) synagogue	10. c) Philippi
b) Philippi	b) three	d) Thessalonica
5. a) Silas	8. a) Scriptures	11. a) first
b) Thessalonica	b) Christ (Messiah)	b) Luke
6. a) 100 miles	9. Corinth	12. Corinth
b) Egnatian Way	10. a) suffered	13. Greeks
c) Macedonia	b) outrageously	

14. Among the converts in Thessalonica were two young men who later became Paul's traveling companions: they were called Secundus and _____ (the two from Thessalonica in Acts 20:4).

15. As Paul later reminded them in the Thessalonian letter, he had presented the gospel to them with power and the Holy Spirit and with complete conviction of its truth (1 Thess. 1:5). So these two young men were deeply impressed: they heard and accepted the message not as a a) _____ word but as the word of b) _____. (1 Thess. 2:13)

16. Aristarchus, from Thessalonica, became one of Paul's outstanding helpers. On the third missionary journey, for example, he was seized by the a) _____ (Acts 19:29) in b) _____ (see the title above Acts 19:23) and barely escaped with his life.

17. Later, among the delegates who accompanied Paul on his journey to Jerusalem with his "help for the poor", we find that Aristarchus (and Secundus) were representatives of the church in _____ (Acts 20:4).

18. When Paul was taken by ship to Rome as a prisoner, he was again accompanied by a) _____ (Acts 27:2), the Macedonian from Thessalonica. The "we" in Acts 27:2 reminds us that b) _____ was also on board. On this journey they were all c) _____ (Acts 27:41) off the coast of d) _____ (Acts 28:1).

19. Finally, in a letter Paul wrote from prison (probably in Rome) we see that both Aristarchus and Luke were still among Paul's a) _____ _____ (Philemon, verse 24) and in another letter we see that Aristarchus was actually in b) _____ with Paul (Col. 4:10).

20. So Luke gives us these delightful thumbnail sketches of Aristarchus, his and Paul's traveling companion. Here they are (but not in order):

    a) Being shipwrecked with Paul.   Picture _____

    b) Being mobbed in Ephesus.   Picture _____

    c) Imprisoned with Paul.   Picture _____

    d) A delegate with aid for the poor in Jerusalem.   Picture _____

    The following drawings are in the right order. Study them now and then write the appropriate letter by the side of each title above. (**Note:** Aristarchus is in white.)

Answers

14. Aristarchus	17. Thessalonica	19. a) fellow workers
15. a) human	18. a) Aristarchus	b) prison
b) God	b) Luke	20. a) C
16. a) people	c) shipwrecked	b) A
b) Ephesus	d) Malta	c) D
		d) B

21. From this, we can see that both the first two churches Paul established in Macedonia, that is
    a) _____ and b) _____, played a big part in his future ministry.

22. **To Think And Pray About:** Read 1 Thessalonians 1:1 to 2:2.

    a) What does this passage teach us about how Paul's visit to Thessalonica affected the lives
       of the people there?

    b) How does the example of Aristarchus confirm what Paul says here about the new Christians
       in Thessalonica?

    c) How much of this has happened to you since you became a Christian? How much more of
       it should you seek? Pray about this.

23. Now review until confident and then do Test 4A. Continue on with Lesson 4B.

Answers

21. a) Philippi
    b) Thessalonica

Lesson 4B

Paul in Thessalonica: Jason's House

(Acts 17:5–10)

> *Read Acts 17:5–10 (Mark the place with a piece of paper). Especially note how Paul's letters agree with Luke's account in the Acts and fill in many important details for us.*

1. While Paul and Silas were in Thessalonica they stayed in the house of _____ (Acts 17:7).

2. Again it is from Paul's two letters to the Thessalonians that we find out more of what they did while they were in Jason's house. Rather than be a burden on Jason, they a) _____ (1 Thess. 2:9) both day and night, suffering toil and hardship. He tells us this again in his second letter to them where he says that they did not *"eat anyone's food without* b) _____ (2 Thess. 3:8) *for it."*

3. Remember that when Paul wrote these letters to the Thessalonians he was in the city of a) _____ (Review), and there he did the same, earning his living by making b) _____ (Acts 18:3).

4. As they lived such a short time in Thessalonica, it must have been very difficult to pay their own way just by making tents. It is interesting to see, therefore, that when Paul wrote later to the Philippian church, he thanked them for sending him help more than once when he was in _____ (Phil. 4:16).

5. So clearly, while Paul was in Jason's house in Thessalonica, he paid his own way; supporting himself by

    a) earning his own living by making _____.

    b) gifts from the church in _____.

6. One day Jason's house was attacked by a dangerous mob of a) _____ _____ (Acts 17:5), stirred up by the jealous b) _____.

Answers

1. Jason
2. a) worked
   b) paying

3. a) Corinth
   b) tents
4. Thessalonica

5. a) tents
   b) Philippi
6. a) bad characters
   b) Jews

---

7.   This mob came in search of a) _____ and b) _____ (Acts 17:4–5) but, failing to find them, they dragged c) _____ (Acts 17:6) and some other believers with him before the d) _____ _____, accusing them of sedition.

8.   From his letter to the Thessalonians we can see that he had taught them about God's a) _____ and glory (1 Thess. 2:12). So now the mob accused Paul of trying to set up another b) _____, called c) _____ (Acts 17:7), in opposition to d) _____, the Roman Emperor. Once again we see how exactly Paul's letter agrees with Luke's account in the Acts.

9.   This accusation created a a) t_____ (Acts 17:8) but eventually they let b) _____ (Acts 17:9) and the others go, but only after they had posted c) _____.

10. In view of this uproar, the Christians thought it best to send Paul and Silas away, so as soon as it was a) _____ (Acts 17:10) they slipped out of Thessalonica and went to the city of b) _____ (Acts 17:10), marked by the Letter c) _____ on the map on the Title Page of Lesson 4A, about 50 miles along the Egnatian Way.

11. Now look back to the pictures on page 9. The one that represents Paul's time in Thessalonica is Picture _____.

12. **To Think and Pray About:**

     Read 1 Thessalonians 2:3–13.

     a)   How much do these verses teach us about what happened during Paul's visit to Thessalonica?

     b)   What can we learn about how we should behave toward others, from Paul's example?

13. Don't forget to do Test 4B and then Lesson 4C before the Group Meeting.

Answers

7. a) Paul
    b) Silas
    c) Jason
    d) city officials
8. a) kingdom
    b) King

8. c) Jesus
    d) Caesar
9. a) turmoil
    b) Jason
    c) bond

10. a) night
    b) Berea
    c) R
11. B

Lesson 4C
Group Study

Paul's Letters to Thessalonica and His Preaching There
(1 and 2 Thessalonians)

We are going to look at the two letters Paul wrote to Thessalonica to see some of the interesting things they can teach us about the tremendous effect Paul's preaching had on the people there.

A. WHAT Paul preached about while in Thessalonica

1. **Review**

    a) In which verse in Acts 17 does Luke tell us what
        Paul preached about in Thessalonica?   v. _____

    b) What did he preach about?

    _____

2.

    Remember that from Macedonia Paul went on to Achaia. Here he wrote two letters back to Thessalonica.

    a) In which city in Achaia did Paul write these two
        letters to Thessalonica, according to the picture?   _____

    b) Who were the joint senders with Paul of these letters?

    _____

3. Now from the two letters Paul wrote to the Thessalonians we can learn a lot more about **"what"** Paul had preached when he was there, because on a number of occasions he refers to this. So let's study these passages now.

a) Look, for example, at 1 Thessalonians 2:12.

What kind of lifestyle had he urged them to adopt when he had been preaching and teaching in Thessalonica?

_____

b) Furthermore, in his preaching in Thessalonica, what kind of lifestyle did Paul say was worthy of God, according to each of the following verses?

1) 1 Thess. 3:3–4 _____

_____

2) 1 Thess. 4:2–8 _____

_____

3) 1 Thess. 4:11 _____

_____

4. It is important to see that each of the truths we looked at in Frame 3 were things **Paul preached about in Thessalonica**. We know this because in each case he says so! In each passage,

a) find the phrase in your Bible where Paul tells us he preached this truth when he was in Thessalonica. You will find these in:

1) 1 Thess. 2:12   2) 1 Thess. 3:4   3) 1 Thess. 4:2, 6   4) 1 Thess. 4:11

b) underline these phrases in pencil.

c) write "P" in the margin, to remind you that Paul preached about this in Thessalonica.

5. Now let's look at his second letter and read 2 Thessalonians 2:5 which is another of the "**what I preached about when I was in Thessalonica**" passages.

Exercise

Underline this verse and mark it with "P".

What did Paul tell them to remember from what he had preached about when he was in Thessalonica? Look back in this chapter to find out.

_____

6. So from both the Acts and Paul's letters we can find out a great deal of what he preached about in Thessalonica. For example, from all these passages we can see that Paul's preaching covered two main areas:

A. Doctrine, especially truth about Jesus.

B. Christian living, based on this doctrine.

To sum up, gather together all he said about A; then about B.

A. _____

_____

_____

B. _____

_____

_____

_____

_____

The letters also tell us:

B. HOW Paul preached when he was in Thessalonica

7. **"How"** did he preach, according to 1 Thessalonians 2:4?

_____

_____

8. So in preaching, Paul had one purpose: to please God and to say only what God wanted, rather than to try to please people (1 Thess. 2:4). This meant that Paul was able to avoid lots of the pitfalls into which so many preachers fall today. Read carefully 1 Thessalonians 2:3–7.

In which verse does Paul mention, or hint at, each of the following pitfalls for those involved in Christian ministry?

Pitfalls for Christian Living and Ministry

a) Try to trick people into the Kingdom with gimmicks.   v. _____

b) Please people with our own cleverness.   v. _____

c) Entice them with flattery.   v. _____

d) Motivated by greed.   v. _____

e) Impress with our status.   v. _____

f) Lack gentleness (a bullying attitude).   v. _____

9. How did Paul (and, by following his teaching and example, how can we) avoid these pitfalls, according to 1 Thessalonians 1:5a?

_____

_____

_____

C. How Paul, the Preacher, LIVED in Thessalonica

10. Now no one could possibly accuse Paul of preaching for money or for his own advantage (as a mere cover up for greed, 1 Thessalonians 2:5). Why? Read 1 Thessalonians 2:9.

_____

_____

11. So Paul could preach in the power of the Holy Spirit because his preaching was **reinforced by a lifestyle which was consistent both with his message and with that of Jesus, his master.**

    a)   What did Paul himself say about his lifestyle? 1 Thessalonians 1:5b.

    _____

    b)   How did Paul live among the Thessalonians, as all could witness? 1 Thessalonians 2:10.

    _____

    c)   What **two** lovely examples does Paul use in 1 Thessalonians 2:7–12 to show how sacrificially he lived among the Thessalonians?

    _____

12. So Paul did not preach in order to be financed by his admirers, but rather in order to serve them more humbly, just as Jesus did.

    But perhaps the passage that tells us most about what kind of person Paul was, although indirectly, is 1 Thessalonians 5:14–25. In telling the Thessalonians how he would like them to be, Paul unconsciously tells us what he himself was striving to be: it was a kind of unconscious self-portrait.

    Find all the things that this passage shows us Paul was like, or aimed at being like, in his own life.

    _____

    _____

    _____

    _____

    _____

    _____

    _____

    _____

    _____

    _____

D. WHAT EFFECT Paul's preaching had in Thessalonica

13. So Paul's preaching was in the power of the Spirit and backed by a lifestyle that was utterly consistent with his message. No wonder they accepted it. How did they accept it? (1 Thess. 2:13)

    _____

14. Now read 1 Thessalonians 1:6–8 and list the things that happened to the Thessalonians because they accepted the message as being from God.

Do we see this kind of thing today? If not, why not?

_____

_____

_____

_____

_____

_____

15. Please will someone read the following passages without comment and then we will pray about it: 1 Thessalonians 1:3, 9, 10 and 1 Thessalonians 5:23–24

16. When you get home, please do:

a) Test 4C.

b) Lessons 5A and 5B, which will tell us how Paul moved on to Berea, and then to Athens. Review the lessons well before doing the tests.

c) Then do Lesson 5C.

Lesson 5A

Berea: Journey to Athens

(Acts 17:10–15; 1 Thessalonians 3)

1. In this lesson we are going to see Paul's visit to Berea, and the two especially good things for which we can remember the Bereans:

    a) their daily study of the Scriptures.   Letter _____

    b) their accompanying Paul in his flight to Athens.   Letter _____

    Study the pictures below and then write the letter of the appropriate picture by each phrase above.

A

B

(Answers on next page)

A. The Bereans study the Scriptures daily

Read Acts 17:10–12, and compare with Picture "A" in Frame 1.

2. You will remember that Luke and Timothy had stayed behind to help the new Christians in a) _____ . So when Paul arrived in Berea he was only accompanied by b) _____ (Acts 17:10). However, we can see from Acts 17:14 that by the time Paul left Berea not only Silas was with him but also c) _____ , who had obviously followed them on from d) _____ .

3. As usual, when they arrived in Berea, they went straight to the a) _____ (Acts 17:10). Here the Jews were different in Berea from those in Thessalonica, being of more b) _____ _____ (Acts 17:11). In order to find out if what Paul had said was true they examined the c) _____ (Acts 17:11). They were so much in earnest that they did this d) _____ _____ (Acts 17:11). As a result many of them e) _____ (Acts 17:12).

4. Now turn back to page 9. The picture that represents Paul's time in Berea is Picture _____ .

B. The Bereans accompany Paul in his escape to Athens

Read Acts 17:13–15 and compare with Picture "B" in Frame 1.

5. Once again Paul had to flee for his life, leaving Berea when unbelieving a) _____ , who had followed him from b) _____ , began stirring up trouble.

6. Paul's two companions, a) _____ and b) _____ (Acts 17:14), stayed on in c) _____ for a time. However Paul left, accompanied by some of the new Christians from the church in d) _____ (Acts 17:15).

7. First, they fled to a Macedonian town on the a) _____ (Acts 17:14) where they could take a boat to the great city of b) _____ (Acts 17:15) in the province of c) _____ ; Paul was still accompanied by the Christians from d) _____ (Acts 17:15).

8. Now here we must turn to Paul's letters to fill in the picture. Read 1 Thessalonians 2:17–20. From these verses we can see that while Paul was waiting on the Macedonian coast, he hadn't wanted to go on to Athens, but rather to go back to see the church in a) _____ (1 Thess. 2:17–18). However this had been impossible because he had been stopped from doing so by b) _____ (1 Thess. 2:18). This we don't learn from Luke's account in the Acts, but by comparing what Paul says in his first letter to the c) _____ .

9. When Paul says that Satan stopped them from returning to Thessalonica, he is probably referring to the fierce opposition of the unbelieving Jews from _____ (Acts 17:13) that Luke speaks about in the Acts. Once again see how closely Paul and Luke agree.

Answers

1. a) A b) B	3. c) Scriptures	6. a) Silas	7. c) Achaia
2. a) Philippi	d) every day	b) Timothy	d) Berea
b) Silas	e) believed	c) Berea	8. a) Thessalonica
c) Timothy	4. C	d) Berea	b) Satan
d) Philippi	5. a) Jews	7. a) coast	c) Thessalonians
3. a) synagogue	b) Thessalonica	b) Athens	9. Thessalonica
b) noble character			

10. So as Paul was unable to return to the church in Thessalonica, he took a ship to the city of a) _____ (Acts 17:15), in the province of Achaia. Thus, Paul arrived in this renowned city, the capital of ancient Greece and the onetime center of Greek art and culture, still accompanied by the Christians from the new church in b) _____ (Acts 17:15) in the province of Macedonia. Thus Paul passed into a new province.

11. Look carefully at the following map and illustrating pictures: read thoughtfully the two passages from 1 Thessalonians which tell us a lot more about what happened.

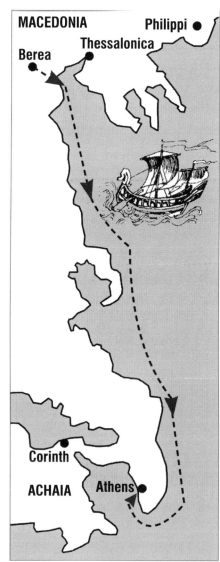

Read 1 Thessalonians 2:17–20 where Paul describes his thoughts on the Thessalonians while waiting on the Macedonian coast with his Berean friends.

Read 1 Thessalonians Chapter 3, where Paul describes his thoughts on the Thessalonians after he arrived in Athens with his Berean friends.

Answers

10. a) Athens
    b) Berea

To Think About

Paul's deep concern for the new Christians in Thessalonica.

Do you share this concern for new Christians?

a)   What did Paul do about it?

b)   What more could you do along these lines?

12.   Now do Test 5A before completing Lesson 5B.

Lesson 5B

Paul in Athens

(Acts 17:15–34)

A. Paul's message to Silas and Timothy from Athens

Read Acts 17:15.

1. So Paul arrived in the greatest city of ancient Greece, which was called a) _____ (Acts 17:15); it was in the province of b) _____ (Review). Here he sent a message back to Silas and Timothy asking them to c) _____ him as soon as possible. This message he sent with the Christians who had accompanied him all the way from d) _____ (Acts 17:14) in Macedonia.

2. Now read 1 Thessalonians 3:1–6. Here Paul describes to the Thessalonians how concerned he was about them while he was in the city of a) _____ (1 Thess. 3:1). Indeed he was so concerned that, much as he wanted b) _____ and c) _____ to be with him (Acts 17:15), he was willing to stay on alone and asked d) _____ (1 Thess. 3:2) to make another visit to the church in e) _____ to help them, and to bring him news of them. Luke doesn't mention this, so we have to complete our picture by seeing what Paul wrote in his letter to the f) _____.

3. This additional information, that we learn from Paul's letter, tells us that Timothy was sent back to a) _____, in order to encourage the church there and find out about their b) _____ (1 Thess. 3:2, 5).

4. We read in Acts 18:1, 5, that Timothy and Silas returned from a) _____ to meet up with Paul again, this time in b) _____.

B. Paul's testimony in Athens

Read Acts 17:16–21.

5. As Paul waited for Silas and Timothy to come to him in a) _____ (Acts 17:16), he spent the time having a good look around this incredible city. There were the most beautiful buildings and statues everywhere, but Paul became more and more b) _____ as he saw how many c) _____ there were everywhere.

6. However this spurred him into action and he began preaching everywhere about a) _____ (Acts 17:18) and the b) _____.

Answers

1.	a) Athens	2.	d) Timothy	4.	a) Macedonia		
	b) Achaia		e) Thessalonica		b) Corinth		
	c) join		f) Thessalonians	5.	a) Athens		
	d) Berea	3.	a) Thessalonica		b) distressed		
2.	a) Athens		b) faith		c) idols		
	b) Silas			6.	a) Jesus		
	c) Timothy				b) resurrection		

7. We see from Acts that Paul testified about Jesus and the resurrection in three different places. These were

    a) the _____. (Acts 17:17a)

    b) the _____. (Acts 17:17b)

    c) the city council, called the A_____. (Acts 17:19)

8. Here are pictures of these three places, look at them carefully and try to work out which is which.

    a) The **synagogue** is marked by the star of David, so this is Picture _____.

    b) The **marketplace** is Picture _____.

    c) The **Areopagus**, probably the hilltop meeting place of the city councilors, is Picture _____.

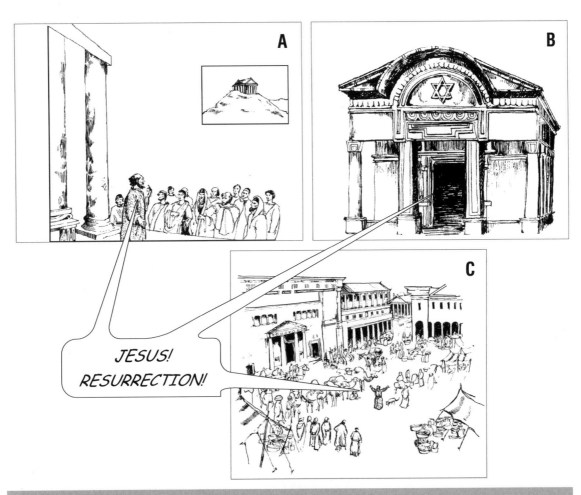

Answers

7. a) synagogue
    b) marketplace
    c) Areopagus

8. a) B
    b) C
    c) A

9. Acts 17:22–31 gives us one of the sermons Paul preached in Athens. We will pass over this now because we will be studying it in our next Group Meeting. However we should notice that of these three places where Paul testified, he actually preached this sermon in front of the a) c_____ c_____ in the b) _____ (Acts 17:22).

10. So if we look back to the pictures on page 9 you will see that the one that represents Paul's stay in Athens is Picture _____.

C. The results of Paul's sermon in Athens

Read Acts 17:32–34.

11. We will finish this study by considering two of the people who were converted on hearing this sermon. One of these people was actually a member of the a) _____ (Acts 17:34), and his name was b) _____; the other was a woman, called c) _____ (Acts 17:34).

12. From Athens Paul went on to the town of a) _____ (Acts 18:1), also in the province of b) _____, from which town he wrote his two letters to the c) _____.

13. On finishing this lesson, do Test 5B. Then go on to prepare for the Group Meeting by doing Lesson 5C.

Answers

9. a) city council
   b) Areopagus
10. D
11. a) council
    b) Dionysius
    c) Damaris

12. a) Corinth
    b) Achaia
    c) Thessalonians

Lesson 5C
Group Study

Paul Preaching in Athens
(Acts 17:16–34)

1. So Paul arrived in Athens, the greatest city of ancient Greece; a center of philosophy, learning and religion. What an opportunity for the gospel of Christ! First, notice the movements of Silas and Timothy in **Acts 17:15–16** (when Paul was in Athens) and in **Acts 18:5** (when he had moved to Corinth).

   Look back to the pictures in Lesson 5A.11 and after reading again what Paul wrote to the Thessalonians in 1 Thessalonians 3:1–5, discuss the reasons for Silas and Timothy's delay in rejoining Paul, and also the points "To Think About" in Lesson 5A.11.

   _____

   _____

   _____

2. Perhaps you have never been alone in a strange city; it's not a very pleasant experience.

   a) What did Paul feel like when alone in Athens after his Berean friends had left? Read Acts 17:16.

   _____

   _____

   b) What comfort would he have got from remembering the Thessalonians? (1 Thess. 1:9).

   _____

   _____

3. Although alone in a strange and rather frightening city, Paul refused to be intimidated.

   What did he do that shows this? Acts 17:17b.

   _____

   _____

   _____

4. What courage to proclaim that Jesus was alive for evermore in such a pagan city as Athens, with its lifeless idols everywhere!

   Read carefully Acts 17:17–19 to find again the three main places where Paul preached.

   Which are these three places? In each case give the verse where it is mentioned and then the letter that marks it in the following picture:

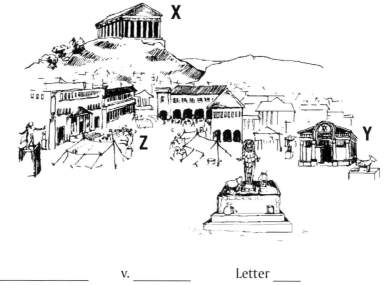

	v. _____	Letter ____
_____	v. _____	Letter ____
_____	v. _____	Letter ____
_____		

✎ **Note:** We follow the traditional view that Paul preached to the city council (the Areopagus) in the magnificent stone building on the top of Mars Hill (Letter X, in the picture). It is possible, however, that he addressed the council in the colonnaded building that you can see in the market square, where they also used to meet.

5. a) What did Paul preach about in Athens? Acts 17:18b.

    _____

    b) Where did he preach this message?

    _____

    _____

6. Read Acts 17:18.

    a) Who debated with Paul?

    _____

    b) How well educated do you think these people were?

    _____

7. Luke gives us a vivid word-picture of the kind of people the Athenians were, in Acts 17:18–23. Read this passage in order to find out which of the following points about the Athenians are correct. In each case give the verse or verses.

    a) They had little education.
    b) They spent all their time in commerce.
    c) They were intellectuals and philosophers.

    d) They were very religious.
    e) They had a real knowledge of God.
    f) They were very ignorant of God.

    __) _____ v. _____

    __) _____ v. _____

    __) _____ v. _____

8. **Review**

Which of the previous three correct answers is represented by each of the following pictures?

A. _____

B. _____

C. _____

9. So the people Paul preached to in Athens were educated philosophers, very religious, but very ignorant of God. Thus in his message Paul gives them a wonderful picture of the true God. In particular he tells them the following six things about God.

   Read carefully this message in Acts 17:24–31 and discuss and note down the verses in which he mentions each of the following things (use all the verses in your analysis):

		Verses
1)	God is creator, and the source of all life.	_____
2)	God therefore wants people to seek and to find him, being very near to each one of us.	_____
3)	But as God is Spirit, his image and nature cannot be represented by any image made by a human being.	_____
4)	So God wants people to repent of such things.	_____
5)	God will one day judge the world by Jesus Christ.	_____ a)
6)	God has proved this, by raising Christ from the dead.	_____ b)

10. **Discussion Point**

    Paul used this simple message to preach the gospel of Jesus Christ to the Athenians. Discuss the importance of each of these six points of Paul's message and how we could use this same message with educated and religious people today who don't know God despite all their knowledge and religion.

    _____

    _____

    _____

11. Now we are going to see what the reaction of the Athenians was to Paul's message, especially about the resurrection.

    Read Acts 17:32–34. There were three reactions to Paul's message. What were they?

    a) _____

    b) _____

    c) _____

12. So it seems that many of the educated, religious Athenians were not very impressed with what Paul said.

    Why is it, we may wonder, that so often highly educated and religious people seem to be such hard ground for the gospel of Jesus Christ when, as we shall see shortly, in Corinth the ordinary and uneducated people flocked to Christ in great numbers? These are matters that Paul discussed in a letter he later wrote to the Corinthians. Read 1 Corinthians 1:18–20 and 1 Corinthians 1:26–31.

    a) In which of these passages does Paul seem to be describing the better educated people, and what does he say about them?

       _____

       _____

       _____

       _____

    b) In which passage does he speak of the ignorant and ordinary people in Corinth, and what does he say about them?

       _____

       _____

       _____

       _____

13. **Exercise**

    Write "like people of Athens" over verse 18 to remind you that this passage speaks of the kind of people Paul met in Athens.

14. From all this Paul came to an astonishing conclusion. Read this in 1 Corinthians 1:21–25.

    a) What is it impossible for people to know by means of their own wisdom?

       _____

    b) What did "wise" people call the message of the cross, that Paul preached?

       _____

    c) But, in God's wisdom, how alone can people be saved?

       _____

15. God is not against education, intellect or people using their minds to the full. But God's wisdom is totally different from this world's wisdom. What are the chief differences according to Paul in 1 Corinthians 2:6–10?

_____

_____

_____

_____

_____

_____

16. So no one can understand anything of God and his salvation without God's Spirit. God's Spirit cannot work to reveal God unless there is a willingness to repent and seek God. What a tragedy that education and intellectual pride should be a barrier to knowing God! The Athenians could not understand Paul and many today cannot for this very reason!

Discussion Point

A    B

Study these two pictures:

a) What does each represent?

b) Why is it so difficult for some intellectual people to be saved?

c) Should Christians reject education and the use of their minds?

d) What is necessary if someone is to understand God's wisdom? Why?

17. Please will someone read Ephesians 1:16–20 without comment. Then let's pray that we may be able to use our minds under the guidance of the Holy Spirit.

18. a) Please do Test 5C after the Group Meeting.

b) Then do Lessons 6A and 6B, which tell us how Paul moved on to Corinth. Review well before doing the tests for these lessons.

c) Do Lesson 6C in preparation for the Group Meeting.

Lesson 6A

Paul in Corinth:
Tentmaker; Evangelist; Letter Writer
(Acts 18:1–8)

> *In Lessons 6A and 6B we will be building up our picture of what happened while Paul was in Corinth by constant reference to*
> *a) the two letters Paul wrote **to** Corinth.*
> *b) the three letters Paul wrote **from** Corinth to other churches, that is:*
> *   • 1 and 2 Thessalonians (during the 2nd missionary journey).*
> *   • Romans (during the 3rd missionary journey).*

1. We will see Paul in three different roles. Study carefully each of the pictures below, and then write the letter of the picture that corresponds to each of his roles.

   a) As evangelist   Picture _____

   b) As letter writer   Picture _____

   c) As tentmaker   Picture _____

A

Silas and Timothy will baptize you.

We believe your message Paul, that Jesus died and rose again to save us and we want to follow him.

B

Please take down a letter for me, Silas and Timothy, to the Church in Thessalonica.

Philippi

Thessalonica

Berea

C

Yes, and it means we meet so many people to tell about Jesus.

Praise God, Aquila and Priscilla, we can work to earn our own living as tentmakers.

And we don't have to burden church funds.

In this lesson we will see Paul in each of these roles, so let's look at the first one:

Answers on the next page/

A. Paul: The Tentmaker (Picture C)

Read Acts 18:1–2.

2. When Paul left Athens, no doubt disappointed by the poor response to his message, he went directly to a) _____ (Acts 18:1). Here he met up and lodged with two Jews called b) _____ and c) _____ (Acts 18:2). These had recently come to Corinth from the city of d) _____ (Acts 18:2), where all Jews had been expelled by the Roman Emperor, e) _____ (Acts 18:2).

3. Aquila and Priscilla earned their living making a) _____ (Acts 18:3), just as b) _____ did, so they worked at this trade together.

4. In his letter to the Corinthians, Paul stressed how important it was to him to earn his own keep. He wrote of his desire to preach the Gospel *"free of* a) _____*"* (1 Cor. 9:18). You will remember that it was just the same in Thessalonica. He wrote to them of how he did not *"eat anyone's food without* b) _____ (2 Thess. 3:8) *for it. We* c) _____ *night and day... so that we would not be a* d) _____ *to any of you."*

B. Paul: The Evangelist (Picture A)

Read Acts 18:4–8.

5. Once Paul had got established, earning his own living, he was able to dedicate each Sabbath (Saturday) to preaching in the Jewish _____ (Acts 18:4) in Corinth.

6. Paul himself later describes what happened: (Read what he says in 1 Cor. 2:1–5) *"I came to you in* a) _____ *with great* b) _____ (1 Cor. 2:3) *and trembling."* He made his message very simple, taking care not to use c) e_____ words (1 Cor. 2:1) and great learning. He concentrated on talking directly about Jesus and especially about his d) _____ (1 Cor. 2:2) on the cross. In this way he made absolutely sure that the faith of the new Christians didn't rest on e) _____ wisdom (1 Cor. 2:5) but rather on the power of f) _____.

7. In all this Paul received a tremendous response to his preaching when the Corinthians began to get news from Thessalonica about the astounding change that had taken place in the lives of those who had become Christians there. Read 1 Thessalonians 1:7-10 to see how Paul describes this: *"not only in Macedonia and* a) _____*"* (1 Thess. 1:8), he wrote back to the Thessalonians from Corinth, *"your faith in God has become known everywhere."* Corinth, of course, was in the province of b) _____, so that is how Paul knew what was going on there.

8. These early days in Corinth, although being low key, were very exciting ones. Two of the first converts in Corinth were a) _____ and b) _____ (1 Cor. 1:14), both of whom Paul promptly c) _____.

Answers

1. a) A	2. e) Claudius	5. synagogue	7. a) Achaia
b) B	3. a) tents	6. a) weakness	b) Achaia
c) C	b) Paul	b) fear	8. a) Crispus
2. a) Corinth	4. a) charge	c) eloquent	b) Gaius
b) Aquila	b) paying	d) death	c) baptized
c) Priscilla	c) worked	e) human	
d) Rome	d) burden	f) God	

9.   As we can see from the Acts, Crispus was the a) _____ of the b) _____ (Acts 18:8) in Corinth, and he believed with all his household.

10. Gaius, a God-fearing Gentile who attended the synagogue in Corinth, was another of the first converts whom Paul a) _____ (1 Cor. 1:14). Soon the new church in Corinth began meeting in his house. We know this because Paul, when writing some time later **from Corinth**, sends greeting to the Christians in Rome from his host in Corinth, called b) _____ (Rom. 16:23), in whose house the c) _____ (in Corinth) met.

11. It seems possible that Paul's host was known by different names: a) _____ in Acts 18:7, whereas in Romans 16:23 he was known as b) T_____ J_____ (Rom. 16:23). Thus his full name could have been c) **G**_____ **T**_____ **J**_____ . His house was next door to the d) _____ (Acts 18:7).

12. Up until now Paul had been alone in Corinth. At long last he was joined by a) _____ and b) _____ (Acts 18:5) who had come down from the province of c) _____ (Acts 18:5).

13. Now you will remember that Paul mentioned in his letter to the Philippians how they had already sent him help a number of times when he was in a) _____ (Phil 4:16). But also they sent help after he had left b) _____ (Phil. 4:15); in other words after he had reached the province of c) _____ . The two who must have brought this money to Paul in Corinth, in Achaia, were d) _____ and e) _____ (Acts 18:5).

14. Furthermore it seems that with the arrival of these reinforcements, Paul must have stopped a) _____ (1 Cor 1:14) the new converts himself; apparently the two younger men, that is b) _____ and c) _____ (Acts 18:5), must have taken over this part of the ministry, leaving Paul with the task of preaching the d) _____ (1 Cor 1:17). As we see in Acts, Paul now had much more time to e) _____ (Acts 18:5) the message.

15. Paul was not only delighted with the gift from Philippi, but also with the excellent news that a) _____ (1 Thess. 3:6) brought him about the b) _____ and c) _____ (1 Thess. 3:6) of the Christians in the church in Thessalonica. This excellent news rekindled within Paul's heart a great desire to d) _____ (1 Thess. 3:10) them again. Now read Paul's description of this joyous reunion with Timothy and Silas in 1 Thess. 3:6–11.

C. Paul: The Letter Writer (Picture B)

16. So on the arrival of Silas and Timothy in Corinth with such wonderful news about the church in Thessalonica, Paul rushed off a letter: from "a) _____, b) _____ *and* c) _____ (1 Thess. 1:1). *To the church of the* d) _____." Thus we have this beautiful first

Answers

9. a) ruler or leader	11. c) Gaius Titius	13. a) Thessalonica	14. c) Timothy	16. a) Paul
b) synagogue	Justus	b) Macedonia	d) gospel	b) Silas
10. a) baptized	d) synagogue	c) Achaia	e) preach	c) Timothy
b) Gaius	12. a) Silas	d) Silas	15. a) Timothy	d) Thessalonians
c) church	b) Timothy	e) Timothy	b) faith	
11. a) Gaius	c) Macedonia	14. a) baptizing	c) love	
b) Titius Justus		b) Silas	d) see	

letter to the Thessalonians which, as we have been seeing, tells us so much about Paul's recent visit there and of the church that he established. We must remember that this letter was written from the city of e) _____ during the f) _____ missionary journey (Review).

17. However, among all this cause for rejoicing, there was one bit of especially sad news from Thessalonica. Since the time when Paul had been with them, several of the Christians there had a) "_____ *in* _____" (1 Thess. 4:13), and their death had made the church b) _____ (1 Thess. 4:13); so Paul hastens to comfort them.

18. Read 1 Thessalonians 4:13–18, where Paul writes from Corinth to comfort the Thessalonians in their bereavement. As regards those who had died believing in Jesus, Paul reminds them of the glorious truth that, after the sound of God's a) _____ call (1 Thess. 4:16), the Lord Jesus himself will come down from b) _____ and those who have died believing in Christ will c) _____ first.

19. Then all the Christians who are alive at the time of Christ's coming again will also be gathered up to meet the a) _____ in the b) _____ (1 Thess. 4:17) and so we will be with the c) _____ for d) _____.

20. What a wonderful reunion that will be! No wonder Paul urges the bereaved Christians in Thessalonia to a) _____ (1 Thess. 4:18) one another (or **comfort** one another) with this wonderful hope of the Lord's b) s_____ c_____.

21. **To Think About**

    Read again 1 Thessalonians 4:13–18. How could you use this teaching to comfort a Christian friend in time of bereavement?

22. **Review:** The sad news that Paul received from Thessalonica was that certain Christians there had a) _____. The glorious truth about Jesus that Paul used to comfort them in their bereavement is of the Lord's b) _____ _____.

23. **Review:** Paul finished this lovely letter to the bereaved Christians in Thessalonica and quickly sent it to them. Remember, then, that this letter was written from the city of a) _____ at the end of Paul's b) _____ missionary journey, and was triggered off by the news brought to him there by c) _____ and his companion d) _____ on coming to him from the province of e) _____. In the next lesson we will learn how Paul also wrote a **second** letter to the Thessalonians from the same city of f) _____, about a year later.

Answers

16. e) Corinth	19. a) Lord	20. a) encourage	23. a) Corinth
f) second	b) air	b) second coming	b) second
17. a) slept/ death	c) Lord	22. a) died	c) Timothy
b) grieve	d) ever	b) second coming	d) Silas
18. a) trumpet			e) Macedonia
b) heaven			f) Corinth
c) rise			

Lesson 6B

The Church in Gaius' House
2 Thessalonians Written

(Acts 18:5–8)

1. **Review**

   As we saw in the last study, things were developing well in the synagogue in Corinth:

   • Paul was well established in his trade of making a) _____.

   • Several Corinthians had accepted Christ and had been b) _____.

   • Paul had been rejoined in Corinth by c) _____ and d) _____.

   • They had brought him fresh financial help, from the church in e) _____.

   • He had been greatly cheered by the good news Timothy had brought about the constancy of the Christians in f) _____.

   • In response Paul had, from Corinth, written and sent off his first letter to the g) _____.

2. Now in this study we will see Paul (still in Corinth):

   a) writing a second letter to the Thessalonians.   Picture _____

   b) preaching in the house of Gaius Titius Justus.   Picture _____

   Look carefully at the following pictures and then write the letter of the picture that illustrates each of the titles above.

Continued/

Answers		
1. a) tents	2. a) B	
b) baptized	b) A	
c) Silas		
d) Timothy		
e) Philippi		
f) Thessalonica		
g) Thessalonians		

B

A. The Church in Gaius' House

Read Acts 18:5–8

3. Things seemed to be going well when suddenly the storm broke! Once more the unbelieving Jews began a fierce persecution, so Paul turned to the a) _____ (Acts 18:6) and withdrew to the house which was next door to the b) _____ (Acts 18:7), that belonged to one of the new converts called c) _____ (Rom. 16:23) Titius Justus. The leader of the synagogue himself, called d) _____ (Acts 18:8), who had been converted with all his e) _____, also accompanied him.

4. As soon as the news got out that Paul had withdrawn from the Jewish synagogue and was preaching daily in the house of Gaius, the Gentiles flocked to hear him. Many believed and were a) _____ (Acts 18:8), not by b) _____, but by c) _____ and d) _____, who were kept very busy! (Review)

B. Paul writes a Second Letter to Thessalonica

5. Month followed month, the church growing all the time. One day fresh news about the Thessalonian church arrived in Corinth. Read 2 Thessalonians 1:1–4.

    According to the new report the faith of the Thessalonians had a) _____ (2 Thess. 1:3) so much, and their b) _____ (2 Thess. 1:3) for one another was growing too. Paul was overjoyed, and just kept c) _____ (2 Thess. 1:3) God all day long.

6. What especially thrilled Paul was the fact that apparently the Thessalonians had suffered the most terrible a) _____ and b) _____ (2 Thess. 1:4) and yet they had continued to believe and to c) **p**_____ (2 Thess. 1:4) through it all.

Answers

3.	4.	6.
a) Gentiles	a) baptized	a) persecutions
b) synagogue	b) Paul	b) trials
c) Gaius	c) Silas	c) persevere
d) Crispus	d) Timothy	
e) household	5. a) grown	
	b) love	
	c) thanking	

7. Once again Paul, from far off Corinth, rushed off a letter: "a) _____, b) _____ *and* c) _____. To the church of the d) _____" (2 Thess. 1:1), he starts.

8. In this second letter Paul had some of the strongest words of condemnation he had ever written for those who were persecuting the Thessalonians. Read 2 Thessalonians 1:5–12.

   Here he says their persecutors will be punished with everlasting a) _____ (2 Thess. 1:9) and separated from the presence of the Lord. This terrible punishment will take place when the Lord Jesus b) is _____ from c) _____ (2 Thess. 1:7) with his powerful d) _____ (2 Thess. 1:7), and in e) _____ _____ (2 Thess. 1:7) to punish these persecutors. What a terrible day that will be for those who make Christians f) _____ (2 Thess. 1:5) for their faith.

9. But on the day of Christ's second coming those who believe will be a) _____ in him and will b) _____ at him (2 Thess. 1:10).

10. **Review**

    In his **first** letter to the Thessalonians Paul tells them of the second coming of Christ to comfort them when their loved ones had a) _____ (Review). In his **second** letter to the Thessalonians he uses the message of Christ's second coming to reassure the Christians who were being b) _____ (Review). In both cases, and in **both** these letters to the Thessalonians one of the main things Paul teaches them is about the c) _____ _____ of Christ (Review). Remember that both these lovely letters to the Thessalonians were written in the city of d) _____, on the e) _____ missionary journey.

11. But apart from those who were **persecuting** the Christian Thessalonians there were troublemakers of a far more dangerous kind, who were subtly teaching false doctrine by saying that the Day of the Lord (that is the day of the second coming of Christ) had already _____ (2 Thess. 2:2).

12. It is quite likely that those who were listening to these errors were saying to themselves: "If Christ has already come, or is about to come in the very near future, why bother to work any more?" Read 2 Thessalonians 3:6–12. Certainly there were those in the church who were living a) _____ lives (2 Thess. 3:11). How glad Paul now was that he had worked and toiled b) _____ and c) _____ (2 Thess. 3:8) to earn his living both in Thessalonica and Corinth. Certainly no one could call Paul d) _____ (2 Thess. 3:7), so he could safely urge them to follow his example. Indeed, when Paul was in Thessalonica he had taught them that *"The one who is unwilling to* e) _____ *shall not* f) _____.*"* (2 Thess. 3:10)

    Clearly those who claim to be too "spiritual" to work are being disobedient to God's word.

Answers

7. a) Paul	8. d) angels	10. a) died	12. a) idle
b) Silas	e) blazing fire	b) persecuted	b) night
c) Timothy	f) suffer	c) second coming	c) day
d) Thessalonians	9. a) glorified	d) Corinth	d) idle
8. a) destruction	b) marvel	e) second	e) work
b) revealed		11. come	f) eat
c) heaven			

13. **To Think About and Do**

    Read 2 Thessalonians 3:6–12 once again.

    A very common attitude is to think that hard work and toil are "unspiritual".

    • How had some of the Thessalonians fallen into this trap?

    • How might we fall into the same error today?

    • What clear teaching does Paul give them and us on the subject?

14. In any case these people were also wrong in thinking that the Lord's coming had taken place or was just about to take place. Paul says clearly that the Day of the Lord will not come until two things have happened: Read 2 Thessalonians 2:1–12.

    First, the final a) _____ (2 Thess. 2:3) (or total apostasy in the church) will have taken place.

    Second, the b) _____ (2 Thess. 2:3) will have appeared.

15. The "man of lawlessness" or "lawless one" seems to be the Antichrist mentioned in other parts of the New Testament. He is someone who will make the false claim that he is a) _____ (2 Thess. 2:4). He will come with the power of b) _____ (2 Thess. 2:9) and perform all kinds of displays of c) _____, d) _____ and e) _____ (2 Thess. 2:9), and use every kind of f) d_____ (2 Thess. 2:10) on those who are g) _____ (2 Thess. 2:10). However Christians need not be afraid because when Jesus does come back again he will overthrow him with the breath of his mouth and h) _____ him (2 Thess. 2:8) by the splendor of his coming.

16. Now one way in which these troublemakers might have tricked the Thessalonians into believing these errors was by pretending falsely that Paul himself had taught these same errors in a a) _____ (2 Thess. 2:2b). It looks as if they had even gone so far as to forge a letter in Paul's name. That is why Paul made sure that in future they would not be deceived by forged letters, by signing every letter with greetings from b) _____ (2 Thess. 3:17), in his c) _____ hand. Praise God we have in our New Testament the genuine letters that Paul himself wrote.

17. **To Think About**

    Read 2 Thessalonians 2:13–17.

    List some of the wonderful things God had in store, not only for the Thessalonians, but for us today.

18. Do the tests for these lessons and then do Lesson 6C.

Answers

14. a) rebellion	15. d) signs	16. a) letter
b) man of lawlessness or lawless one	e) wonders	b) Paul
	f) deceit	c) own
15. a) God	g) perishing	
b) Satan	h) destroy	
c) power		

Lesson 6C

Group Study

Christ's Second Coming

(1 and 2 Thessalonians)

> *In our Group Study today we will take a closer look at the truth that is **central** to **both** Paul's letters to the Thessalonians, that is, Christ's second coming. We will look at three key passages on this.*
> *A. 1 Thessalonians 4:13–18.*
> *B. 2 Thessalonians 2:1–10.*
> *C. 1 Thessalonians 5:1–8.*

A. Read 1 Thessalonians 4:13–18

Now, basing your answers on the passage you have just read, do Section A (that is, Nos. 1 to 7 following).

1. When Paul wrote his first letter to the Thessalonians there was a major problem in the church. From the Thessalonians' problem we will learn something of tremendous importance which should spur us on in our Christian lives.

   a) What was this problem?

   _____

   b) What does Paul say in v.14, to comfort them in this problem?

   _____

   _____

2. **Exercise**

   Underline verse 13 in your Bible to remember this problem in the Thessalonian church. Then draw a line down the margin of verses 13 to 18 of 1 Thessalonians 4 to remind you how Paul comforted them.

3. a) Whose teaching is Paul talking about?

   _____

   b) What of those believers who are alive on the "day of the Lord"?

   _____

4. **"The day of the Lord"**

   This is a phrase used in the Bible to speak of God's final act of judgment and salvation. In the New Testament it refers to the day when Christ will come again, save his people and establish his Kingdom forever.

   a) What are the signs for the Lord's return?

   _____

   b) What will happen to those who have died?

   _____

   c) What will happen to those who are living?

   _____

   d) What will be the final outcome for all believers?

   _____

5. Using 1 Thessalonians 4:15–17, you should be able to explain the events of the Lord's return. Please can someone read out the following sentence, filling in the blanks by saying the missing words.

   The _____ of the Lord will begin with a loud _____, the dead will _____ to _____ and those who are still alive (Christians) will be _____ up to meet the Lord. So we will be with the Lord _____. Paul tells us this in _____.

6. **Exercise**

   Write **S.C.** in the margin of 1 Thessalonians 4:16–17 to remember that in these verses Paul teaches about Christ's Second Coming in power.

7. **Discussion**

   Exchange any ideas you had on 6A.21 ("To Think About").

B. Read 2 Thessalonians 2:1–10

Base your answers to this Section B (Nos. 8 to 16 below) on this passage.

8. You will remember that in Lesson 6B we saw that some of the Christians in Thessalonica had become thoroughly confused about Christ's second coming, probably because of a forged letter they had received in Paul's name. That is why Paul wrote his **second** letter to them and signed it with his **own** hand. So let's see what we can learn about this confusion.

   What were they confused about?

   _____

   _____

9. **Exercise**

   Underline 2 Thessalonians 2:2 to remember the error that some people were spreading about Christ's Second Coming and write **S.C.** in the margin.

10. What two things will happen before Christ returns?

_____

11. **Exercise**

    Draw a circle around the words **"man of lawlessness"** (or **"lawless one"**) in 2 Thessalonians 2:3.

12. **"Man of Lawlessness" or "Lawless one"**

    We cannot be certain what Paul meant by this phrase (at least not at the present time). But Scripture (Paul's letter) tells us what this person will be like. His personality fits that of an agent of Satan, in other parts of the Bible called the Antichrist. What will the "man of lawlessness" do?

    _____

13. a) Why hasn't this happened yet?

    _____

    b) When will it happen?

    _____

14. In what way will the lawless one's coming be revealed and with whose power?

    _____

    _____

15. There is a saying. "The darkest hour precedes the dawn." It will be so in the world just before Christ returns. But what will Christ do when he comes?

16. **Exercise**

    2 Thessalonians 2:8 is the "key" verse in this passage — a bright star shining in a very dark sky, so underline it and write **S.C.** in the margin.

    ## C. Read 1 Thessalonians 5:1–8

17. **Discussion**

    a) Why doesn't the householder notice the thief's entrance into the house?

    _____

    b) Why won't the world notice the Lord's approach in the same way?

    _____

18. a) What does Paul call the period before Christ's second coming

    1) for Christians? _____

    2) for non-believers? _____

    b)   What is the future after Christ's second coming:

       1)   for Christians? 1 Thess. 4:17   _____

       2)   for non-believers? 1 Thess. 5:3   _____

19. **Discussion**

    a)   How many of you believe that Jesus Christ could come again during your lifetime?

    b)   What will Christ's return mean for your family, friends and neighbors (salvation or destruction)?

    c)   Who is responsible for telling them of Christ before he comes?

    d)   How should the near return of Christ effect our Christian witness and that of our church?

    e)   Are we really concerned about others' situation in eternity?

20. Will someone read Romans 13:11–14 without comment.

Now let's pray, asking the Lord to help us to be more alert ourselves and to waken others from their spiritual sleep, in view of the nearness of the Lord's coming.

21. When you get home:

    a)   Do Test 6C after the Group Meeting.

    b)   Do next week's Lessons, 7A and 7B, which cover Paul's final period in Corinth before his return journey home. After reviewing each lesson do the respective tests.

    c)   Then do Lesson 7C.

Lesson 7A

Vision of Christ in Corinth
Gallio's Judgment

(Acts 18:9–17)

1. In this lesson we will see two more important events that took place while Paul was in **Corinth**.

   a) The vision of Christ   Picture _____

   b) Gallio's favorable judgment   Picture _____

   Study the two pictures below and then write the letter of the correct picture by the side of each title above.

A. Vision of Christ in Corinth

Read Acts 18:9–11 and compare with Picture "A" in Frame 1.

2. When Paul had been forced out of the synagogue in Corinth by the persecuting Jews he must have felt very discouraged. It was then he suddenly saw the a) _____, in a b) _____ (Acts 18:9) in the night.

3. It was just like the vision on the Damascus road all over again; Jesus coming to him to reassure him in his distress. Jesus told him not to be a) _____ (Acts 18:9) nor give up, but keep on b) _____ because he was still with him. He gave Paul a promise: there would be many converts in the city of c) _____. Now look back to the pictures on page 9. The one that represents Paul's time in Corinth is Picture d) _____.

4. It was just what Paul needed. Exhausted by his long journey, discouraged by being constantly hounded by the unbelieving Jews, his own body stiff and weary from the beatings he had received in Philippi and elsewhere, Paul must have been tempted to give up. Now it was different — Jesus had appeared to him again with encouragement and clear instructions. So Paul stayed on in Corinth for a a) _____ and a _____ (Acts 18:11) teaching the people the b) _____ of _____.

B. Gallio's Favorable Judgment

Read Acts 18:12–17 and compare with Picture "B" in Frame 1.

5. But the unbelieving Jews were not going to give up. One day they suddenly seized and dragged Paul before the Roman place of a) _____ or court (Acts 18:12), accusing him of breaking the Jewish b) _____ (Acts 18:13) in his teaching of the people.

6. Now in God's plan, a most noble and upright man had just been appointed Roman proconsul in Achaia. His name was a) _____ (Acts 18:12). Paul was just about to defend himself when the Roman proconsul himself cut the proceedings short by saying that he was not prepared to b) _____ (Acts 18:15) a case about petty differences on matters of the Jewish c) _____. Gallio then had the Jews d) _____ away from the court (Acts 18:16).

7. This was a historic occasion. For the first time a Roman Court had pronounced in favor of Christianity and come down on the side of a) _____ against the persecuting b) _____.

8. It is important that the Bible student should know something of what secular historians outside the Bible can tell us about Gallio. This provides us with excellent background information. So read the contents of the following Panel and then continue with Frame 8.

Answers

1. a) A	3. c) Corinth	6. a) Gallio
b) B	d) E	b) judge
2. a) Lord	4. a) year and a half	c) law
b) vision	b) word of God	d) driven
3. a) afraid	5. a) judgment	7. a) Paul
b) speaking	b) law	b) Jews

LUCIUS JUNIUS GALLIO

From fragments of documents found in Delphi in Greece in 1905 we know that Lucius Junius **Gallio** was installed as Proconsul (Roman governor) of Achaia on July 1, 51 A.D. and held this office for two years. He was the brother of Seneca the well known Roman philosopher and favorite of the Roman Emperor Claudius. Seneca wrote of Gallio his brother: "None is so pleasant to anyone as Gallio is to everyone."

According to the above panel we can see that Gallio was an agreeable kind of person. He was also a man of high standing, as his brother was none other than a) _____ (Panel) who in turn was a favorite of the Roman Emperor, b) _____ (Panel). Gallio was appointed governor of Achaia in the year c) _____ A.D. and held office for d) _____ years. We know this from fragments of documents found in Greece in 1905, in the town of e) _____ .

9. Now to get back to our story; the Corinthians were so angry with the Jews for persecuting Paul like this that they seized the new leader of the synagogue, called a) _____ (Acts 18:17), who had obviously taken the place of b) _____ (Acts 18:8) when he became a Christian, and they c) _____ (Acts 18:17) him in front of the d) _____ . But e) _____ just ignored it, probably thinking it would teach him a sharp lesson.

10. We need to repeat that this was a truly key point in history as it was the first time a Roman court had protected the Christians. Possibly Paul remembered this incident when he wrote favorably about civil authorities in his letter to the Roman church, while in **Corinth**, some six years later, saying: a) _____ (Rom. 13:3) are not to be feared by those who do right, because they are God's b) _____ (Rom. 13:4), working for our own good.

11. So with this favorable court ruling by the governor himself, the top Roman official in Achaia, Paul and his team were able to move freely through the whole province preaching openly about Jesus.

    We know that a new church was established in the neighboring seaport of a) _____ (Rom. 16:1), so Paul most probably preached there. From the way he uses the example of the b) g_____ (1 Cor. 9:25) and of c) f_____ like a boxer (1 Cor. 9:26) it seems possible that they had visited the Isthmian Games (similar to the Olympic games) which were held in A.D. 51, and preached to the vast crowds there.

Answers

8. a) Seneca	9. a) Sosthenes	11. a) Cenchreae
b) Claudius	b) Crispus	b) games
c) 51	c) beat	c) fighting
d) 2	d) court	
e) Delphi	e) Gallio	
	10. a) rulers	
	b) servants	

12. **Review**

So as Paul's time in Corinth drew to an end, as indeed did his a) _____ missionary journey, he had much to praise God for. Many had believed and been baptized in the city of Corinth itself. There was a new church in the neighboring port town of b) _____. Possibly he had preached to the athletes and vast crowds gathered at the c) _____ games. He had written d) _____ letters to the church in Thessalonica and he had obtained a favorable judgment in the court by the Roman proconsul e) _____. Altogether he spent a very fruitful time in Corinth. Above all, Paul himself felt a renewed sense of call because it was in Corinth that f) _____ appeared to him again with encouragement and clear instructions.

13. **To Think and Pray About:**

Read Romans 13:1–7.

a) To what extent do you think Gallio's favorable judgment affected Paul's attitude here to the Roman authorities? Remember, he wrote this letter (Romans) from Corinth where Gallio had been the governor a few years earlier. Do you think Paul had Gallio in mind as he wrote Romans 13:3?

b) What responsibilities do Christians have toward rulers of state (Rom. 13:1) and where do these responsibilities cease (Acts 4:19)?

c) What benefits should these rulers extend to the people?

d) How does Paul's experience in Corinth illustrate the right relationship between church and state?

Other verses on this subject:

Matthew 22:21; 1 Timothy 2:1–3; Titus 3:1; 1 Peter 2:13, 14 and 17.

14. Do Test 7A after reviewing well. Then go on to do Lesson 7B.

Answers

12. a) second
    b) Cenchreae
    c) Isthmian
    d) two
    e) Gallio
    f) Jesus (or Christ)

Lesson 7B

Idolatry and the Permissive Society in Corinth

Review of Paul's Letters that Throw Light on Corinth

I hope by now that you have realized that there are two kinds of letters that can throw light on a town where Paul is ministering:

- Letters he wrote **to** the church in that town from some other place to which he had moved.

- Letters he wrote **from** that town to churches in other places.

As regards **Corinth**, we have learned much from **both** these kinds of letters.

1. For example we can easily tell the letters that Paul wrote **to** Corinth. We have **two** of these in the New Testament and their names give them away. They are:

   a) _____   b) _____

2. Now these are letters that Paul wrote back **to** Corinth after he had left there. We will study these in detail when we come to the **third** missionary journey, when they were written. But what about the letters Paul wrote **from** Corinth on his **second** missionary journey, the journey we are studying now? You should now know that these are his

   a) first letter to the _____ .

   b) second letter to the _____ .

3. In his letter to the Romans Paul sent greetings to them from a man called a) _____ (Romans 16:23), in whose house the b) _____ (Rom 16:23) met. As Gaius was one of the first converts in c) _____ (1 Cor. 1:14) we can see that Paul must have been writing this letter to the Romans when he was in the city of d) _____; but this was later (on his third journey).

4. Most people know which of the New Testament letters Paul wrote to a particular person or church because the names tell us this.

   What students often don't know are the letters Paul wrote **from** those towns or cities nor on which of his missionary journeys he wrote them. To make this clear the Supplement on page 91 tells you the letters Paul wrote on each missionary journey with the town from which he wrote it and Paul's approximate age at the time.

Answers

1. a) 1 Corinthians b) 2 Corinthians	2. a) Thessalonians b) Thessalonians	3. a) Gaius b) church c) Corinth d) Corinth

---

Look carefully at this Supplement. Notice that to the right of each of Paul's missionary journeys you will find: the letters he wrote on that journey, then the place where he wrote them *from*, and finally his approximate age at the time of writing them.

5. According to the Supplement, Paul wrote _____ letters in all.

🖉 **Note**: It's probable that Paul wrote other letters, but these were not kept, and therefore do not form part of the New Testament.

6. Now look again at the Supplement, and notice how

   a) on his **1st** missionary journey Paul wrote only _____ letter.

   b) on his **2nd** missionary journey he wrote _____ letters.

   c) on his **3rd** missionary journey he wrote _____ letters.

🖉 **Note:** It is easy to remember the number of letters he wrote in each journey as they correspond to the journey in question, either 1, 2 or 3.

7. Using the Supplement as our guide we will now look at the journeys one by one. For example, we see that on returning from his **first** journey Paul wrote a letter to the a) _____ (Supplement). He wrote this when he was in the city of b) _____ (Supplement) and at the time when he was approximately c) _____ (Supplement) years old.

8. On his **second** journey he wrote two letters. These were: a) _____ and b) _____ (Supplement). He wrote both of these **from** the city of c) _____ (Supplement) **to** the church in d) _____ (Supplement).

9. On his **third** missionary journey Paul wrote three letters. Two of these he wrote **to** the city of a) _____ (Supplement). The third one he wrote **from** the city of b) _____ (Supplement), when he revisited there; this was his letter to the c) _____ (Supplement).

10. So, of the five letters Paul wrote on his **second** and **third** missionary journeys those he wrote

   From Corinth were a) _____, b) _____ and c) _____.

   To Corinth were d) _____ and e) _____.

11. In other words **all five** of the letters Paul wrote on his **second** and **third** missionary journey were written either **to** or **from** the same city, which was _____.

Answers

5. 13	8. a) 1 Thessalonians	10. a) 1 Thessalonians
6. a) 1	b) 2 Thessalonians	b) 2 Thessalonians
b) 2	c) Corinth	c) Romans
c) 3	d) Thessalonica	d) 1 Corinthians
7. a) Galatians	9. a) Corinth	e) 2 Corinthians
b) Antioch (Syria)	b) Corinth	11. Corinth
c) 49	c) Romans	

12. Look at these pictures about Corinth, and then read Panel "A", below the pictures.

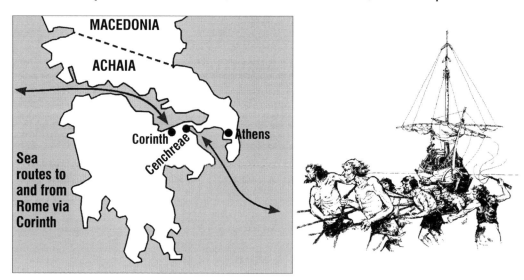

PANEL "A"

Corinth was situated on a narrow isthmus, about five miles wide, pinched between two gulfs, like the extra slim waist of Achaia, which was stormy and dangerous. It was therefore the ideal spot to move merchandise and entire ships, from one gulf to the other, without going all round the southern point of Achaia. Here Paul often saw great gangs of slaves heaving and sweating under the master's lash as they dragged ships on rollers from one sea to the other. All north-south traffic also had to pass through Corinth. Check these points on the map. With about a quarter of a million people drawn from all over the Roman Empire, Corinth was the biggest city Paul had yet tackled; a rootless, restless, seething mass of humanity. What a scene for a new church! What a challenge to the gospel!

13. Now continue, using Panel "A" and the map to answer.

Corinth was situated on the western side of a very narrow strip of land which joined the two land masses of Achaia to the north and south. Such a narrow joining strip of land is called an a) _____ (Panel "A"). This was a strategic situation as it even allowed overland haulage of entire ships, dragged on rollers by teams of b) _____ (Panel "A"), to pass directly from one ocean to the other on their way to or from c) _____ (see map).

The eastern port for this sea traffic, where Paul later established a daughter church, was called d) _____ (Rom. 16:1, also see map). Because of its unique situation, Corinth had mushroomed to become a vast commercial city of nearly e) _____ (Panel "A") inhabitants. It was the capital of the Roman province of f) _____ (see map).

Answers

13. a) isthmus
    b) slaves
    c) Rome

13. d) Cenchreae
    e) 1/4 million
    f) Achaia

14. As in some of our overcrowded inner city areas today, Corinth was a cesspool of vice and urban violence. Paul describes some of the dreadful sights he saw all around him in his letter to the Romans. The people were filled with all kinds of wickedness, evil, greed and a) _____ (Rom. 1:29). They were full of envy, b) _____, c) _____ d) _____ and e) _____ etc. (Rom. 1:29)

15. But of all their terrible evils the one that most stood out was sexual sin. Read what Paul says about this in Romans 1:26–27. Here Paul is describing the sexual perversion of a) h_____. Paul wrote this letter to the Romans when he was in the city of b) _____ (Supplement), so he was only describing what he saw all around him as he wrote. These kinds of things were so bad in Corinth that the early Greek comedians coined the phrase "living like Corinthians" to refer to c) s_____ sins.

16. One of the main reasons Paul had for writing his first letter to the Corinthians was to rebuke and correct just such a sin in the church: one of the church members was actually sleeping with his a) _____ _____ (1 Cor. 5:1). Even worse, instead of being filled with sadness, some of the other church members thought it was a huge joke and were actually b) _____ (1 Cor. 5:2) of it. Paul was absolutely clear this man should be c) _____ _____ (1 Cor. 5:2) of the fellowship.

17. In his letter to the Romans Paul also describes the other great evil in Corinth which, as we shall see in a moment, was very closely linked with these sexual sins. Instead of worshiping the immortal God, they worshiped a) _____ (Rom. 1:23). So it's not surprising that another great evil that Paul had to correct in Corinth was that of food offered to b) _____ (1 Cor. 8:1).

18. Read Panel "B" about idolatry in Corinth filling in the missing word.

PANEL "B"

High up in the mountain that looked down on Corinth from the south, was the great temple of **Aphrodite**, the Greek goddess of the glorification of sex. A thousand girl prostitutes were attached to this idol. Another of the idols in Corinth was **Apollo**, the ideal of male beauty. His temple contained nude statues and pictures of Apollo in postures that inflamed the passions of the men worshipers to acts of homosexuality with the temple boys. No wonder that sexual sins were referred to as

"Living like _____."

Answers

14. a) depravity
    b) murder
    c) strife
    d) deceit
    e) malice

15. a) homosexuality
    b) Corinth
    c) sexual

16. a) father's wife (step-mother)
    b) proud
    c) put out

17. a) images
    b) idols

18. Corinthians

19. Continue using Panel "B" and the pictures above to answer.

    Two of the principal idols of the Corinthians were sex symbols. The **male** sex symbol was the idol called a) _____ (Panel "B") which is Picture b) _____ above. The **female** sex symbol was called c) _____ (Panel "B") which is Picture d) _____ above. In offering sacrifices to them the Corinthians were also indulging in the most dreadful e) _____ orgies.

20. Now we can understand why mention of these two evils, sexual sins and idolatry, are linked together in Paul's letter to the Corinthians. For example we find people who are a) im_____ (1 Cor. 6:9) and people who worship b) _____ rebuked together. Immediately after are mentioned the sins of c) a_____ (1 Cor. 6:9) and d) h_____ (1 Cor. 6:9).

21. The two principal evils that we find rebuked side by side in Corinth are a) im_____ and b) id_____.

22. **To Think and Pray About:** Read Romans 1:18–32.

    Remember that Paul wrote these words from Corinth and was therefore most likely to have been describing the people he saw there. What picture of the Corinthian culture does it conjure up for us? Be ready to discuss this in the next Group Meeting.

    Read Romans 1:16–17. What happened in Corinth, do you think, that can account for Paul's amazing confidence in the gospel against such a terrible background as we see in Romans 1:18 onwards? Compare with Romans 5:20 and 1 Corinthians 1:4–9.

    In our Group Study we will see what Paul taught the Corinthians about the body, sex and God's presence, and how wonderfully his preaching brought hope and victory to people surrounded by such immorality and perversion.

23. Review well before doing the test. Then do Lesson 7C.

Answers

19. a) Apollo	20. a) immoral	21. a) immorality
b) A	b) idols	b) idolatry
c) Aphrodite	c) adultery	
d) B	d) homosexuality	
e) sex		

Lesson 7C
Group Study

Our Bodies, Our Sexuality and God's Presence
(1 Corinthians 5 and 6)

> In this last Group Study we are going to see Paul's attitude to the terribly corrupt moral society in Corinth. So first let's review what we have learned about this, and deepen our knowledge.

A. The Corrupt Society in Corinth

1. As we saw in 7B.22 (To Think About) the thoughtful Bible student can learn so much about Corinth from the letters Paul wrote both **to** and **from** this city. For example, what can you learn about the **corrupt society** in Corinth from Romans 1:23–32, now that you know that Paul wrote these words while he was in Corinth, surrounded on every side by their way of life?

   _____

   _____

   _____

2. By understanding the background in Romans, chapter 1, we get a terrible and vivid picture of the corrupt society in Corinth, the city **from** which Paul was writing this letter. The letters he wrote **to** Corinth confirm this picture. Read 1 Corinthians 5:9–13.

   a) What terrible thing had happened **within** the new church in Corinth, which illustrates this?

   _____

   b) Why didn't Paul condemn Christians for their contacts with immoral **non**-Christians, and what does this confirm to us about the Corinthian society? Compare what Paul says here with how Jesus behaved toward similar people in Matthew 9:10-13.

   _____

   _____

   c) Why then do you think Paul felt that this particular man should be separated from the fellowship of the church for a while?

   _____

   _____

d)   When he really repented, what treatment did Paul recommend for this man, according to his later letter in 2 Corinthians 2:5–10? (It seems likely that Paul is referring to this same man here; but even if it is someone else, the same principles apply)

_____

_____

e)   In view of all these points, sum up what our attitude should be to cases of immorality within the church.

_____

_____

_____

3.   In 1 Corinthians 6:9–20 Paul returns to this theme. Read 1 Corinthians 6:9–11. Notice again how, indirectly, Paul reveals what life was like in Corinth.

a)   Discuss how accurately Paul's description here fits with what we have learned from Romans 1 and with the historical facts we studied in Lesson 7B about the Corinthian culture.

_____

_____

b)   To what extent do these things occur in our contemporary society?

_____

c)   To what extent have they even penetrated **within** the church today, and are **condoned** there?

_____

_____

d)   What transformation had taken place in many of the Corinthians who had become real Christians? Find the three changes that had taken place that Paul especially mentions in verse 11.

_____

_____

_____

B.   The Right and Wrong Uses of our Bodies

4.   Read 1 Corinthians 6:12–20. Paul's message of "being put right with God by faith in the Lord Jesus Christ" which we saw in v.11 was sometimes misunderstood. Christ **did** indeed die for our sins so that we might be freed from its penalty, but some Christians used this as an excuse.

a)   As an excuse for what? (v.12)

_____

b)   What does Paul say against this?

_____

5. In verse 13, Paul speaks of **two** bodily appetites. What are these?

    _____

6. As with all our God-given appetites, we can use them either rightly or wrongly. However, God's purposes are not the same for each of our bodily appetites, and it is important to know how they vary from each other. For example, how does the sexual appetite differ from the appetite for food if we are to use it rightly, according to God's purposes? Compare Matthew 6:11 with Hebrews 13:4.

    _____

    _____

    _____

7. How then do we use each of these appetites **wrongly**? See the example of this in Corinth mentioned in 1 Corinthians 6:9–10.

    On the **wrong** use of our appetite for food see Proverbs 23:21 and Philippians 3:19 (where Paul uses the same word "stomach" as in 1 Corinthians 6:13).

    _____

    _____

    _____

8. To fix in your mind what we have learned, here are two pictures that represent the bodily appetites which Paul mentions here.

    Which man **risks** using his body for wrong reasons?   Picture _____

9. In these matters, Corinth had sunk to the dregs; nothing less than a spiritual miracle could put things right there. Yet Paul believed this could happen; he was not intimidated by the dreadful climate of immorality he found there.

    a) What did Paul believe the gospel to be, even in corrupt Corinth? (See Rom. 1:16)

        _____

    b) Why was he so sure of this? (See 1 Cor. 6:11)

        _____

10. In 1 Corinthians 6:12–20, Paul teaches us four tremendous reasons why our bodies are of such value to God and to us. Once we fully grasp these reasons they will help us not to misuse our bodies, but rather to dedicate them entirely to God's purposes.

What are these four reasons why our bodies are so valuable?

1) In 1 Corinthians 6:13b.

_____

_____

_____

_____

2) In 1 Corinthians 6:14. Compare with 1 Corinthians 15:42–44.

_____

_____

_____

_____

3) In 1 Corinthians 6:15–18.

_____

_____

_____

_____

4) In 1 Corinthians 6:19–20.

_____

_____

_____

_____

11. **Exercise**

    Write the numbers 1, 2, 3 and 4 in the margin of your Bible against these four passages in 1 Corinthians 6:12–20 (as shown in Frame 10, above) to help you to find again these reasons why our bodies are so valuable, and therefore should never be misused.

12. At some time or another we are all attacked fiercely by Satan, and tempted to use our bodies wrongly, even if it is by making a god of our stomachs and of our other bodily desires and comforts. Paul's message is wonderfully contemporary. So to close, will someone please read what he says in 1 Corinthians 10:13 (without comment) and then let's pray together about it all.

13. a) When you get home, after the Group Meeting, do Test 7C.

    b) Next week we will have the Final Exam so it is very important to do Lessons 8A and 8B thoroughly. In them we will see how Paul's **second** missionary journey ended with him giving a report of all he had done on this journey: this will be your opportunity to review all we have learned on

       • Paul's life on his **second** missionary journey.
       • Paul's letters that relate to his **second** missionary journey.

    So review by following the instructions carefully and going over **all** the Tests.

Lesson 8A

Return to Antioch: Report on Second Journey

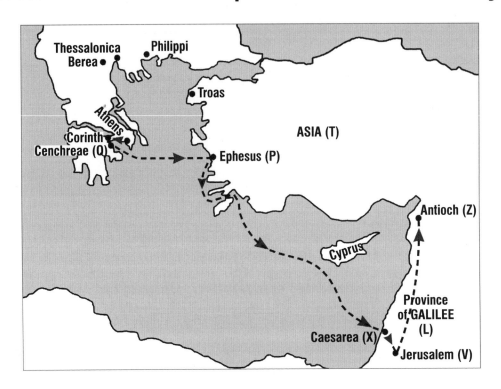

A. Homeward Bound

Read Acts 18:18–22.

1. After Gallio's judgment in his favor, Paul a) _____ _____ (Acts 18:18) a profitable time in Corinth before finally leaving with b) _____ and c) _____. They walked to the nearby eastern port of the isthmus, called d) _____ (Acts 18:18) marked on the map by the Letter e) _____. It seems that either Paul or Aquila had taken a vow (the Greek text is not clear which of the two is meant) and according to Jewish custom, as a sign that the vow had been kept, the one concerned now had his hair f) _____ _____ (Acts 18:18). All this time there, they may have been looked after by g) _____ (Rom. 16:1) who was active in serving the church in h) _____.

2. Then the three boarded a ship; their first port of call was a) _____ (Acts 18:19) marked on the map by the Letter b) _____, where they went and discussed with the Jews in the c) _____.These Jews showed real interest and asked Paul to stay longer,

1. a) stayed on	1. g) Phoebe	
b) Priscilla	h) Cenchreae	
c) Aquila	2. a) Ephesus	
d) Cenchreae	b) P	
e) Q	c) synagogue	
f) cut off		

which he was unable to do. However, he did promise to d) _____ _____ (Acts 18:21) if it were God's will. He also left behind in Ephesus his two friends, e) _____ and f) _____ (Acts 18:19) to carry on until he got back.

3. So Paul sailed on to Palestine, leaving the ship at the port of Caesarea, marked on the map by the Letter a) _____. From there he went directly to b) _____, marked on the map by the Letter c) _____.

4. We will soon see that one of Paul's great concerns during his **third** missionary journey was to make a a) _____ (1 Cor. 16:1) to help God's people in b) _____ (1 Cor. 16:3). It must have been on this visit that Paul was saddened to see so many of the Jewish Christians there so desperately c) _____. As a result God put into his mind the plan to raise "Aid for Jerusalem".

5. It is important to remember that during his **third** missionary journey one of Paul's main interests, which we will see coming up again and again, was his plan to raise "A___ for _____." (Rom. 15:26)

6. A little later, in writing about the 500 people to whom the risen Christ had a) _____ (1 Cor. 15:6) in Galilee (about 20 years before), Paul says that *"most of whom are still* b) _____ (1 Cor. 15:6), *though some have* c) _____ _____." Now in order to have this up-to-date information from Galilee it has been suggested that from Jerusalem Paul could have returned by land to the city of d) A_____ (Acts 18:22) marked on the map by the Letter e) _____, thus passing through the province of f) _____, marked on the map by the Letter g) _____. He could thus have met all these witnesses personally and talked with them with great joy.

7. Once back in his home in Antioch Paul stayed there _____ _____ (Acts 18:23). We may be sure that he would have repeated what he did on returning from his **first** missionary journey, and told the church about all that God had done.

✎ **Note:** So here we come to an end of our study of Paul's **second** missionary journey. Take a few minutes looking at the map on the Title Page of this lesson and following the route Paul took from Corinth back to his home church in Antioch.

B. Paul's Report to Antioch about his Second Journey

✎ **Note:** The rest of this lesson covers Paul's report to the church in Antioch and is a good opportunity for us to **review** many of the main points we have learned: for this reason no references are given.

8. In this second report to the church in a) _____ Paul would have told them of all the wonderful things that had happened on his **second** missionary journey, in Europe, in the provinces of b) _____ and c) _____.

Answers

2. d) come back	4. a) collection	6. d) Antioch
e) Priscilla	b) Jerusalem	e) Z
f) Aquila	c) poor	f) Galilee
3. a) X	5. Aid for Jerusalem	g) L
b) Jerusalem	6. a) appeared	7. some time
c) V	b) living	8. a) Antioch
	c) fallen asleep (died)	b) Macedonia
		c) Achaia

9. He would have told them about the three new churches that had been set up in Europe in the northern province of a) _____; that is, the churches of b) _____, c) _____ and d) _____.

10. Also of the vigorous new church in the great, bustling commercial city on the western coast of the isthmus in the southern province of a) _____; that is, the city of b) _____.

11. For sure he would have told them how on his outward journey he had revisited Lystra in Galatia where a young convert from his first journey had joined his team and whose name was _____.

12. He would have told how he had tried to turn off to his left and visit the province of a) _____, but how he had been prevented by the b) _____ _____. So instead he had pressed on to the coastal town of c) _____ where he had met up with his new companion, called d) _____, who was by profession a e) _____.

13. It was also in this coastal town that Paul had the vision of the man of a) _____ who had called him to come over and help in Europe. The first big city where they stayed was b) _____, which was a c) _____ colony.

14. We can best remember the wonderful events that took place here by thinking about four of the principal people concerned. There was

   • the Jewish woman whose mind the Lord opened, her name was a) _____.

   • the girl from whom Paul drove out an b) _____ _____.

   • the man who was converted after an c) _____, who was the d) _____.

   • and Paul's team member who stayed on seven years, looking after the new church in Philippi; this was e) _____.

15. The next town in Macedonia was a) _____. Here Paul preached in the b) _____ for three sabbaths. Some Jews came to believe, and also God-fearing Greeks and quite a few prominent women. One of the young men converted here became a faithful traveling companion of Paul's: his name was c) _____.

16. However, the hostile Jews mobbed the house of a) _____, where Paul had been staying; so he moved on to another town in Macedonia called b) _____. The people of this town were noted for two things: they searched daily in the c) _____ to find the truth, and several of them who became Christians accompanied Paul all the way to the city of d) _____, after he had escaped from the hostile e) _____ in Macedonia.

Answers

9. a) Macedonia	12. a) Asia	13. c) Roman	15. b) synagogue
b) Philippi	b) Holy Spirit	14. a) Lydia	c) Aristarchus
c) Thessalonica	c) Troas	b) evil spirit	16. a) Jason
d) Berea	d) Luke	c) earthquake	b) Berea
10. a) Achaia	e) doctor	d) jailer	c) Scriptures
b) Corinth	13. a) Macedonia	e) Luke	d) Athens
11. Timothy	b) Philippi	15. a) Thessalonica	e) Jews

17. The first town (or city) that Paul visited in Achaia was a) _____, famed for its Greek culture and intellectual life. Here Paul proclaimed the gospel in three main places which were

     b) the _____.

     c) the _____.

     d) the _____.

18. Here Paul preached his celebrated sermon, but there was a relatively poor response. However we know that several people were converted; among these was a woman called a) _____ and a man called b) _____.

19. The city where Paul stayed longest in Achaia was a) _____. Here Paul worked for his living, as a b) _____, along with a Jewish couple called c) _____ and d) _____. As usual at the beginning he preached in the synagogue, but soon had to withdraw because of the hostility of the Jews and went to the house of Titius Justus also called e) _____, one of the first converts, who was baptized by Paul himself. It was in Corinth that Paul was rejoined by f) _____ and g) _____ who brought good news about the faith of the new Christians in h) _____ to whom Paul wrote i) _____ letters.

20. Corinth was a large city noted for its extreme moral corruption, based on their worship of two sex gods called a) _____ and b) _____. It was in this environment that Paul saw the power of Christ at work; but it was a continual struggle.

21. Perhaps, because of this, one night Paul had a vision of a) _____, who greatly encouraged him. Also it was in Corinth that the Roman proconsul, called b) _____, gave a judgment favorable to Paul against the hostile Jews who had accused him. This favorable judgment in a Roman court was a great step forward for the gospel at this time.

22. Finally, Paul must have reported how, on his homeward journey, when the ship was running down the Asian coast, he had called in at the city of a) _____. Although he had not been able to stop this time, he had left b) _____ and c) _____ there, and had also promised to return later, which he did on his d) _____ missionary journey.

23. Review as usual and then do Test 8A.

24. **VERY IMPORTANT:** To complete your review, go over all the **tests on Lessons "A" and "B"** (1 to 8) until you are sure of all the points we have learned about Paul's **second** missionary journey. Also go over all the **pictures** in this book. You will then be well prepared for Part "A" of your Final Exam which covers this part of Paul's life.

Answers

17. a) Athens	19. a) Corinth	19. h) Thessalonica	22. a) Ephesus
b) synagogue	b) tentmaker	i) two	b) Priscilla
c) marketplace	c) Priscilla	20. a) Apollo	c) Aquila
d) Areopagus	d) Aquila	b) Aphrodite	d) third
18. a) Damaris	e) Gaius	21. a) Christ (or Jesus)	
b) Dionysius	f) Silas	b) Gallio	
	g) Timothy		

Lesson 8B

Review of Paul's Letters

(Connected with His Second Journey)

Instead of the usual study, review thoroughly all the tests on Lessons "C" (Nos.1 to 7) which are at the back of this book. Whenever necessary, look back to the relevant Group Study to refresh your memory on the details. The test for this Lesson 8B will be Part "B" of the Final Exam, which will cover what we have learned about 1 and 2 Thessalonians, 1 Corinthians, Philippians and 1 and 2 Timothy.

The next Group Meeting will include the Final Exam for this course. Please arrive punctually. You will be allowed to use your Bible in the Exam, but not your Student Workbook.

> *Well, I pray that this study of Paul's **second** missionary journey has really been a help to you. I hope that, after a well earned rest, you will go on to complete Paul's Life and Letters by doing Book 3, which majors on his marvelous **third** missionary journey, to Asia (Ephesus), his captivity in Rome, and the respective letters.*

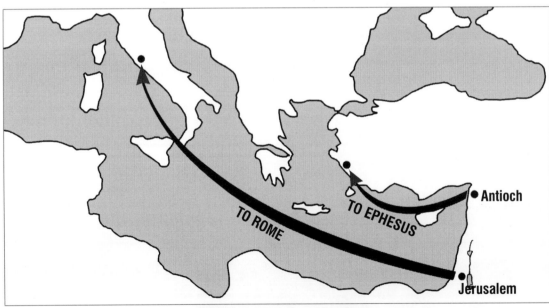

THIRD MISSIONARY JOURNEY

Supplement

Period in Paul's Ministry	Order of Writing	Letter Written		Paul's Approx. Age
First Missionary Journey	1	To: GALATIA	From: ANTIOCH (in Syria) - On returning from Galatia	49
Second Missionary Journey	2	To: THESSALONICA (first letter)	From: CORINTH	51
	3	To: THESSALONICA (second letter)		52
Third Missionary Journey	4	To: CORINTH (first letter)	From: EPHESUS	56
	5	To: CORINTH (second letter)	From: MACEDONIA (return visit)	56
	6	To: ROME	From: CORINTH (return visit)	57
First Imprisonment	7	To: EPHESUS	From: ROME (probably)	61-62
	8	To: COLOSSAE		
	9	To: PHILEMON in COLOSSAE		
	10	To: PHILIPPI		
Period when released	11	To: TITUS in CRETE	?	63-66
	12	To: TIMOTHY in EPHESUS (first letter)		
Second Imprisonment and Martyrdom	13	To TIMOTHY in EPHESUS (second letter)	From: ROME	67

✎ **Note:** Paul's age is calculated here as if he were born in the year 1 A.D. (which can't be far from the mark). Therefore his age at any time corresponds to the date A.D.

These ages (and dates) are, of course, only tentative, but they do give a good general idea of Paul's age at the time of writing.

TESTS

Test for the Introductory Group Study

1. What was the name of the Council's delegate sent
    with Paul who was soon to become his new team
    mate on the second missionary journey?   _____

2. From which church did he come originally?   _____

3. a) What did he carry with him on this journey,
        that supported Paul in his ministry to the Gentiles? _____

    b) On reaching their destination, how did the non-
        Jewish Christians react to this?   _____

    c) In which church did this happen?   _____

Test 1 (A and B)

1. Fill out the following plan with the provinces and five towns connected with Paul's second
    missionary journey, in the order in which he visited them. Each time add the number that
    marks the place on the map below.

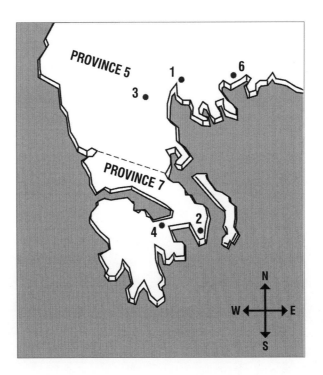

	Name	No. on map
A. **Northern Province:**	_____	_____
Towns: 1.	_____	_____
2.	_____	_____
3.	_____	_____
B. **Southern Province:**	_____	_____
Towns: 1.	_____	_____
2.	_____	_____

2. Write the five chosen "key" events of Paul's second missionary journey in the order in which they occurred.

1) _____

2) _____

3) _____

4) _____

5) _____

How to Do the Tests for the Group Studies on Returning Home

1. Whenever necessary, use your marked Bible to find the places referred to.

2. Try not to look at the Group Study unless you cannot answer.

Test 1C (on Group Study)

1. Recall the five key events (shown in the pictures we saw on page 9) that took place in each of the five towns that Paul visited in Macedonia and Achaia on his second missionary journey. Write these below in the order in which they occurred, giving in each case the town and province.

	Event	Town	Province
1)	_____	_____	_____
2)	_____	_____	_____
3)	_____	_____	_____
4)	_____	_____	_____
5)	_____	_____	_____

(Continued on next page)

2. To which of these towns did Paul write letters which we have in the New Testament and what were these letters?

<table>
<tr><td align="center">**Towns**</td><td></td><td align="center">**Letter or Letters**</td></tr>
<tr><td>_____</td><td>–</td><td>_____</td></tr>
<tr><td>_____</td><td>–</td><td>_____</td></tr>
<tr><td>_____</td><td>–</td><td>_____</td></tr>
</table>

3. a) Write down two of the things that Peter says in the New Testament that show his approval of Paul and his letters:

   1) _____

   2) _____

   b) Now find this passage in your Bible and write the reference. _____

Test 2A

1. Which province did Paul want to revisit when he first set out on his second missionary journey? _____

2. With whom did Paul have a serious disagreement? _____

3. About what person did they disagree? _____

4. Who wanted to take this person on the second missionary journey? _____

5. a) Who did not want to take him? _____

   b) Why not? _____

6. What happened as a result of this argument? _____

7. Whom did Paul take with him on the second missionary journey? _____

8. a) Where did Barnabas go, instead of accompanying Paul? _____

   b) Whom did he take with him? _____

9. What did the church in Antioch do for Paul and his new companion as they set off on the second missionary journey?

_____

Test 2B

1. Name the young Christian whom Paul met again in Lystra. _____

2. What nationality was

    a) his mother? _____

    b) his father? _____

3. a) If a child were born of parents of different nationalities, from which parent did he receive his nationality in Jewish eyes? _____

    b) What nationality was this young man, according to the Jews? _____

4. a) What did Paul do to him? _____

    b) In consideration of whom did he do this? _____

5. What big decision did this young man make? _____

6. a) What did they deliver to the churches? _____

    b) What two beneficial results did this have on the churches?

    _____   _____

7. Name the three members of the missionary band that left Lystra.

    _____   _____   _____

Test 2C

Summarize what you have learned from Paul's letters to Timothy about the way he trained people for the ministry, by answering the following questions. Don't forget, you may use your marked Bible and look back to the Group Study if necessary.

A. The **MAN** Paul trained (Timothy)

Write down any five things we learned about Timothy himself from Paul's letters to him.

References

1) _____   _____

2) _____   _____

3) _____   _____

4) _____   _____

5) _____   _____

(Continued on next page)

B.   The **MATERIAL** used

Give any five examples of the kind of things Paul taught those he was training for ministry.

1)   _____

     _____

2)   _____

     _____

3)   _____

     _____

4)   _____

     _____

5)   _____

C.   The **METHOD** used

1)   What must we do if we are really going to progress in our own training?

     _____

2)   What was the ultimate objective of Paul's on-the-job training course for ministry, which made it such a dynamic and indeed explosive thing?

     _____

Test 3A

1.   a)   In which important province did Paul want to
          preach God's Word on leaving Galatia?   _____

     b)   Who forbade him to do so, on this occasion?   _____

     c)   To which coastal town did they come instead?   _____

2.   What method did Paul use to find God's guidance
     on this occasion?   _____

3.   When Paul reached the coast,

     a)   who joined his party there?   _____

     b)   what was the name of the town where this happened?   _____

     c)   how do we know this person linked up with
          them there?   _____

     d)   what was this newcomer's occupation?   _____

4. a) Who appeared to Paul in this coastal town? _____

   b) In what way did he appear? _____

   c) At what time? _____

   d) To which province did Paul go as a result? _____

   e) What number marks it on the map in Test 1 (A and B)? _____

5. Who was the only writer in the New Testament who was not a Jew? _____

6. Two very important things happened to Paul in the coastal town he came to:

   • He got a new companion.
   • He was called to preach in a new continent.

   a) What was the name of the town where these two things happened? _____

   b) Which number marks it on the map on the Title Page of Lesson 3A? _____

7. a) How many were in the missionary team when they left by ship for a new continent? _____

   b) Who were they? _____

   c) What is the modern name for the new continent to which they sailed? _____

Test 3B

1. a) Name the first city where Paul stayed and ministered in Europe. _____

   b) What is the number that marks it on the map in Test 1 (A and B)? _____

   c) In which province was it? _____

   d) Of which empire was this city a colony? _____

2. a) Where did Paul go to make his first contact with the people? _____

   b) Name the first convert in Philippi. _____

   c) Where did the missionary team stay in Philippi? _____

3. a) Who kept following and upsetting Paul? _____

   b) What did Paul do? _____

   c) What did the enraged owners do? _____

   d) What double punishment did Paul and Silas receive? _____

   e) What did Paul and Silas do, even in this awful situation? _____

(Continued on next page)

3. f) What did God send, to get them out of this situation? _____

    g) Who was converted as a result of this? _____

4. In the case of the two people we are told were converted,

    a) what step did both take, immediately after their conversion? _____

    b) in each case, who took this step with them? _____

5. Why were the Roman authorities so frightened by what they had done to Paul?

_____

6. a) Name the members of the missionary team who arrived in Philippi.

_____

    b) Name the two members who now left Philippi together. _____

    c) Of the two who stayed on, name the one who looked after the new Christians while Paul was away and until he revisited there on his third missionary journey. _____

    d) How do we know this? _____

7. Where did Paul next stop, after Philippi? _____

Test 3C

A. **WHEN** the Philippians supported Paul.

Below are listed the five main occasions when the Philippians sent support for Paul and his ministry. Find in your Bibles the reference for each:

1) On the very first day of their conversion. _____

2) Several times when he was in Thessalonica. _____

3) Again when he arrived in Corinth (Achaia). _____

4) The aid fund for the poor in Judea. _____

5) When he was in prison (probably in Rome). _____

B. **HOW** the Philippians supported Paul.

Write any three of the outstanding things about the way the Philippian church gave support to Paul and his ministry, with the references.

1) _____ _____

2) _____ _____

3) _____ _____

Test 4A

1. a) When Paul left Philippi, which of his companions accompanied him? _____

    b) What was their next stopping point? _____

    c) What number marks this place on the map in Test 1 (A and B)? _____

    d) In which province was this town? _____

2. a) Where did Paul first go to preach the gospel? _____

    b) How many weeks did he stay there? _____

3. a) Name the young man in this town who became a Christian through Paul's preaching and later became one of his traveling companions on his journey to Rome. _____

    b) In later years, in which city was this person seized by an angry mob? _____

    c) What disaster did this man suffer with Paul, on his journey to Rome? _____

    d) What further injustice did he later suffer with Paul (probably in Rome)? _____

4. a) In which of Paul's two letters, that he later wrote to the Thessalonians, did he describe his complete physical exhaustion when he arrived in Thessalonica? _____

    b) According to this letter, what had happened to him to cause this exhaustion?

    _____

    c) Where did this happen, according to this same letter? _____

    d) From which city did Paul later send both his letters to the Thessalonians? _____

Test 4B

1. In whose house did Paul stay while he was in Thessalonica? _____

2. Paul paid for his keep while he was there. What two sources of income did he have in order to do this?

    _____   _____

3. a) Who attacked the house where Paul and Silas were staying? _____

    b) Who encouraged them in this? _____

4. a) Whom did they find in the house? _____

    b) Whom did they fail to find? _____

(Continued on next page)

5. a) Before whom did they drag their captives? _____

   b) What did these captives have to do in order to obtain their release? _____

6. a) Where did Paul and Silas go now? _____

   b) When did they leave Thessalonica? _____

Test 4C

What do we learn from Paul's letters to the Thessalonians about the following matters?

1. What did Paul preach about when he was there? Write down three of the main things. In each case try to find the supporting verse or verses.

   References

   1) _____   _____

   2) _____   _____

   3) _____   _____

2. How did Paul preach when he was there?

   _____

3. How did Paul, the preacher, support himself when he was in Thessalonica?

   a) _____

   b) _____

4. What effect did Paul's preaching have on the Thessalonians? Mention 3 of the main things.

   1) _____

   2) _____

   3) _____

Test 5A

1. a) Who arrived in Berea with Paul? _____

   b) Who joined them shortly after, from Philippi? _____

2. How did the Jews in the synagogue in Berea differ from those in Thessalonica? _____

3. a) Where did they look in order to find out if
   what Paul was saying was true? _____

   b) How often did they do this? _____

   c) With what result? _____

4. a) Who were the people who made Paul flee from Berea? _____

   b) From which town had they come? _____

5. a) Who stayed on in Berea for a while? _____

   b) Who accompanied Paul on his journey? _____

6. a) Where did Paul really want to go, when he got
   to the coast of Macedonia? _____

   b) Who stopped him? _____

   c) To which city did he go instead? _____

   d) In which province was this? _____

   e) Who accompanied him? _____

Test 5B

1. a) Who did Paul send back to Berea from Athens?

   _____

   b) What message did they take back to Silas and Timothy? _____

   c) Which church did Timothy have to visit first? _____

   d) In which letter does Paul tell us this? _____

   e) Because of this delay, where did Silas and
   Timothy eventually catch up with Paul? _____

2. a) In which province was Athens? _____

   b) What upset Paul so much about Athens? _____

3. a) Name the three places where Paul witnessed in Athens.

   _____ _____ _____

   b) In which of these did Paul preach his sermon
   recorded in the Acts? _____

(Continued on next page)

4. Name the convert in Athens who was

   a) a member of the city council. _____

   b) a woman. _____

5. a) To which town did Paul go, on leaving Athens? _____

   b) In which province was this? _____

Test 5C

1. Write down any three of the important things that Paul said to the Athenians in his message on the Areopagus; give the reference for each.

   References

   1) _____ _____

   2) _____ _____

   3) _____ _____

2. Name the three important things that describe the Athenians, as seen in the following verses:

   1) _____ Acts 17:18

   2) _____ Acts 17:22

   3) _____ Acts 17:23

3. In which passage in 1 Corinthians does Paul describe

   a) the false wisdom of the well-educated Athenians and their like? 1 Cor. 1: _____ – _____

   b) the way God has called mainly simple people to faith in Christ? 1 Cor. 1: _____ – _____

Test 6A

1. To which city did Paul go when he left Athens? _____

2. With whom did Paul lodge in Corinth? _____

3. a) How did Paul make his living while he was in Corinth? _____

   b) Who else there had the same trade? _____

   c) From which city had this couple come? _____

   d) Which Roman Emperor had turned all the Jews out of that city? _____

4. a) Where did Paul start preaching in Corinth? _____

    b) What did he especially preach about? _____

5. Two of the early converts were Gaius Titius Justus and Crispus.

    a) What important office did Crispus hold before
        he was converted? _____

    b) What important service did Gaius render the
        Corinthian church? _____

    c) Who baptized these two early converts? _____

6. a) Who arrived to help Paul in Corinth? _____

    b) What part of his ministry did they take over from him? _____

    c) From which province had they come? _____

    d) From which church did they bring financial aid? _____

    e) What was Paul now able to spend more of his
        time doing, as a result of all this? _____

7. a) From which church did Timothy bring good news? _____

    b) Which letter did Paul write on receiving this news? _____

    c) In which city was Paul when he wrote this letter? _____

    d) On which of his missionary journeys did he write this letter? _____

8. a) What sad thing had happened in Thessalonica
        since Paul had left there? _____

    b) What great truth about Jesus did Paul tell them
        in order to comfort them? _____

Test 6B

1. a) When the unbelieving Jews in Corinth began
        persecuting Paul, to whom did he begin to preach instead? _____

    b) By the side of which building was the house
        where Paul now began to preach? _____

2. a) Once Silas and Timothy arrived in Corinth,
        what part of the ministry did they take over from Paul? _____

    b) What did Paul concentrate on, instead? _____

(Continued on next page)

3. Two of the new Christians were Crispus and Gaius Titius Justus.

    a) Which of these had previously been the leader of the Jewish synagogue? _____

    b) And which opened his house for Paul's preaching and for the church to meet? _____

    c) Who baptized them both? _____

4. a) What was happening to the Thessalonian Christians at this time?

    _____

    b) How were they reacting to this? _____

5. a) What were some false teachers in Thessalonica saying about Jesus' second coming? _____

    b) What error of behavior had resulted from this? _____

6. So Paul wrote his second letter to the Thessalonians to correct these errors.

    a) In explaining that Christ had not yet come, whom did Paul say must come first? _____

    b) What false claim will he make? _____

    c) What will the Lord Jesus do to him when he does come back again? _____

7. Remember that Paul taught this in his second letter to the Thessalonians.

    a) From which city did he write this letter? _____

    b) On which of his missionary journeys did he write this letter? _____

8. a) In this second letter to the Thessalonians, what did Paul do, so that they could be sure that he had written it?

    _____

    b) Why did he do this?

    _____

Test 6C

1. a) Which truth about Christ does Paul especially emphasize in both his letters to the Thessalonians? _____

    b) Give one reference as an example. _____

2. a) What error were some people spreading around about this great truth? _____

    b) Give the reference where Paul mentions this. _____

3. Paul corrected this error by telling them that someone was going to appear first.

    a) What does he call this person? _____

    b) Give the reference where Paul names this person in this way. _____

4. a) On the day of the Lord, what will Christ do to this person? _____

    b) Give the reference for this. _____

5. Paul wrote his first letter to the Thessalonians to comfort them after a great sorrow.

    a) What was this sorrow? _____

    b) In which verse in 1 Thessalonians does Paul speak of this? _____

Test 7A

1. a) When Paul had been forced out of the synagogue in Corinth, he must have wondered if the Jews would ever allow him to establish a church. What happened to reassure him in his depression?

        _____

    b) So how long did Paul go on preaching in Corinth? _____

2. a) What was the name of the Roman proconsul of Achaia who was appointed while Paul was in Corinth? _____

    b) What relationship did he have with Seneca, the famous Roman philosopher and intimate friend of Claudius, the Roman emperor? _____

    c) In which year was he appointed? _____

    d) What was found in Delphi that gives us this exact date? _____

3. a) Who dragged Paul before this Roman proconsul? _____

    b) In whose favor did the Roman proconsul give his judgment? _____

    c) In order to teach the Jews a lesson, who did some of the Corinthians beat up in the clear sight of the Roman proconsul? _____

    d) How did the proconsul react to this? _____

    e) Why was this judgment so important? _____

4. a) In which neighboring port town was a daughter church planted? _____

    b) In what public place did Paul probably preach to vast crowds of Corinthians? _____

Test 7B

1. a) How many letters did Paul write on his second missionary journey? _____

    b) Which were these? _____

    c) From which city did Paul write these two letters? _____

    d) What other letter did he also write from this same city, but on a later journey (the third)? _____

2. a) How many of Paul's New Testament letters were written from Corinth? _____

    b) Name them. _____

    c) How many did he write to Corinth? _____

    d) Name them. _____

3. a) Where was Corinth situated, that made it especially important? _____

    b) Name the port which gave Corinth access to the sea on the east? _____

    c) What was Corinth especially notorious for, morally? _____

4. Of the two "sex" gods in Corinth that we have seen in this lesson,

    a) which was the goddess? _____

    b) which was the male god? _____

5. In Romans 1, Paul gives us a terrible picture of both idolatry and sexual sin side by side in Corinth. How do we know that Paul was describing here what he was seeing all around him at the time he was writing?

    _____

6. a) With whom had one of the church members in Corinth been sleeping, that illustrates to us the appalling immorality of the city? _____

    b) How did many of the Corinthian church react to this sin at first, thus showing us just how low their moral standards were in that city? _____

    c) What did Paul say they must do with this man?

    _____

    d) With what other evil were the sex sins especially linked? _____

Test 7C

1. a) Which chapter in Romans gives us a terrible
        picture of the corrupt moral climate that prevailed in Corinth?   _____

    b) How do we know that in this passage Paul must have been describing the sins that
        abounded in Corinth?

        _____

    c) Name two of these sins he mentions.   _____ and _____

2. Describe the four tremendous reasons Paul gives in 1 Corinthians 6 that show how valuable
    our bodies are in God's sight, with the reference for each.

                                                                        References

    1) _____   _____

    2) _____   _____

    3) _____   _____

    4) _____   _____

Test 8A

1. a) From which port did Paul leave Achaia?   _____

    b) Name the Christian couple who accompanied
        him at this time.   _____

    c) What did Paul (or possibly his companion) do in
        this town, before taking ship?   _____

    d) Who would have looked after them while they were there?   _____

2. a) What important city did Paul visit on his sea trip back to Palestine?   _____

    b) In which province was this city?   _____

    c) Who did he leave there as a kind of advance party?   _____

(Continued on next page)

3. In which town and province did each of the events occur, which are shown in Pictures "A" to "E" on page 9? In each case give the letter that marks it on the map below.

	Town	Province	Letter
A.	_____	_____	_____
B.	_____	_____	_____
C.	_____	_____	_____
D.	_____	_____	_____
E.	_____	_____	_____

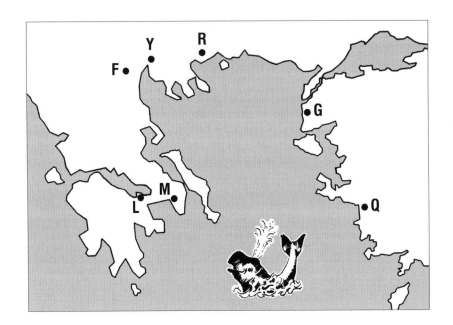

4. a) Name the town where Paul met Luke, and give the letter that marks it on the map above.   _____ _____

    b) Name the town Paul visited in Asia on his homeward journey and give the letter that marks it on the map.   _____ _____

HAS THIS COURSE BEEN A BLESSING TO YOU?

WOULD YOU LIKE TO BE A BLESSING TO OTHERS?

SEAN is a small missionary organization that reaches out through its courses to more than 100 countries in over 80 languages. Using our materials, national Christians reach areas where foreign missionaries cannot venture.

Please consider now if you would like to help others by praying and supporting our ministry. You can find out more about SEAN International and the courses which are available by visiting our website:

www.seaninternational.org or by email to **contact@seaninternational.org**